Sheila McGlarry

In Mourning...
The Loss of a Living Child

Sheila McGlarry

Copyright © 2013

All rights reserved. No part of this book maybe reproduced or utilized in any form or by any means without written permission by the author.

ISBN-13: 978-1480123885

ISBN-10: 1480123889

Sheila McGlarry

Dedicated to all the lost souls of the world and the mother's who love them.

Sheila McGlarry

"It's easier to build strong children than to repair broken men."

~Frederick Douglass

Chapter One

As I stumbled across the bedroom floor in the dark following the sound of the ringing phone on my desk, my voice cracking, I managed to say, "Hello?" The other end of the line was silent for a moment and I was about to hang up, thinking someone either dialed the wrong number or was playing a prank to wake me up, then hang up, but then I heard my son Joey's voice, "Mom?" He paused. My brain instantly knew something was wrong. Maybe he was drunk or maybe he just needed to talk. "I'm sorry. I didn't mean for this to happen. I don't even know how to tell you this, but I'm at a police department on Long Island. The police arrested me for burglary. Mommy, I'm really sorry. My bail is $10,000.00. Can you come here? I'm sorry, Mom. I know I have to get my life together. I don't even know how I got to this point. Can you come bail me out?"

As I was listening, trying to rationally absorb his words, holding myself up with one hand on the desk, I felt my heart quickly sinking as I searched for the chair to sit on in the darkness; I felt my legs weakening beneath me. My eyes focused on the clock, the numbers that glowed neon green read five after four in the morning. My brain was scrambling to sort out the words he was speaking though my mind kept repeating, "burglary," "burglary," "burglary. " My body quickly numbing, all I could say was, "What burglary?"

Your brain knows what it is hearing, but there is no way logically in your mind that this is your life happening at this moment or more so your son's. You see your child's life crashing before your eyes and you are helpless. You have always felt helpless, and now the impact of everything you thought you did wrong, or didn't do, or should have done, is also crashing down, down around your world, down around your heart, crashing down.

Joey had been out on Long Island, N.Y. working in magazine sales, a traveling position which he took to get away from home in Peekskill, just north of N.Y.C. for a while. His life, he felt, had been going nowhere and this job he saw as an opportunity for him to get out into the world, meet new people and make a clean, fresh start where no one could judge him. I had at this point thrown him out for the third and final time at the young age of 20. So, when he took this job in spite of my reservations, I thought it might possibly be good for him. On the rare occasion when he had a job, he couldn't seem to hold on to it, so at worst I thought he would just quit and walk away from this one with an excuse, as he usually did.

He preferred to do nothing but hang out with his friends drinking, and getting high. This may be why he felt his life was not where he wanted it to be. I was hoping this job would give him some insight in to life. I was hoping he would be around people who might influence him to strive for more and that maybe he would want to try and achieve more for himself. I was hoping he would have an epiphany and be brave enough, strong enough to be able to make the necessary changes.

He went on with his explanation to me as to why he got arrested; he said that a woman to whose home he had gone to sell a magazine subscription, told him after a short conversation if he needed anything, to come back to her house. He said it was hot and the van had dropped a bunch of guys off, he was thirsty and thought of her kindness, he went back hoping to use her phone to be able to call the driver of the van to come pick him up. He said he had been knocking on the door for five minutes and no one was answering the door, which was slightly ajar, so he went inside. He said he was calling for her but she did not respond so he decided to use the phone anyway. He went on to say there was money on the table next to the phone and he made the choice to take it.

Listening intently to every word he was saying, I was trying to envision his actions in my mind, the boldness he felt in entering a stranger's home. I sat there in the chair, in the dark, staring at the clock, my heart sinking even more deeply into my chest. I started to cry.

I thought at this very moment life had taken yet another turn onto that steep bend that is just so hard to turn around from. Was I having a bad dream? I had seen more than enough people go down Unknown Avenue. His life would forever be altered from this action. Most likely all of our lives would be.

"Joey, what were you thinking? I don't even know what to say right now. I just can't believe this is happening." My thoughts went to his bail being $10,000.00

He didn't answer except to say he wanted to put an officer on the phone, who subsequently gave me some bits of information. The officer told me Joey was being charged with burglary, which is a felony. He told me that my son had taken money from the woman's home. He gave me the information as to which court he would be arraigned in and he said I could have a minute with Joey and then he would have to be processed.

Joey got back on the phone and he asked me if I would come out to Long Island, which was a little over an hour away. I told him I couldn't. I couldn't even think straight, never mind waking his brothers up and driving out there with them in the car at four in the morning. I told him he needed to keep it together and let's see what happens when he gets arraigned. He hung up on me.

He hung up on me... I sat there at my desk overwhelmed, crying.

I prayed to the Lord and asked Him what this child was thinking. I prayed that he gave me strength. The sadness that crept over me filled my body with every breath I took.

How could I begin to deal with this? I couldn't even process what was happening. I had no clue what the future would hold for him. I was scared to death that it was going to be dim and bleak. I couldn't fathom at that moment in time just how tumultuous and heartbreaking our future was about to become.

I walked out into the lightly lit hallway and went down the hall into one bedroom where my son A.J., at the precious age of eight, was sleeping soundly. I bent over him and kissed his round cheeks and told him how much I love and adore him. I started to cry, remembering when Joey was like this, so innocent, so sweet…unaware of cruel challenges and evil temptations that neither one of us thought he might ever have to endure.

I went to the bedroom next to his, where my other son, Anthony, was sleeping. I walked over to the side of his bed and adjusted the covers over him. I thought, "This is the age when Joey started to go wrong on me. Fourteen should be an age where boys are discovering girls, enjoying sports and video games, not smoking marijuana and drinking alcohol." I kissed him and told him how much I love and adore him, except I added that every time he turns around I will be standing right there behind him. I told him I will be on his backside so much that he will think it is just his own shadow behind him.

My legs still weak and shaky, I went back to my own room and lay back down on the bed. I thought of my son in a cold jail cell and I kept replaying his words in my mind. I cried, not quite believing this was happening. Then I realized the one thing he did not tell me was how he had gotten caught.

How was he discovered? Was the woman in the shower and came out to see a strange man standing there? Was she doing laundry unaware, not paying attention to the odd sounds in her home? Was she walking down the hallway and suddenly stopped dead in her tracks out of shock to see a six-foot-tall man in front of her?

I couldn't help but wonder what this woman was thinking in the very first few precious moments when she realized there was a man standing there in her home, and then when she realized he looked familiar. What was she thinking in the seconds that you tell yourself to be calm, the instant before panic kicks in? Was she petrified? Did her knees buckle? Was her heart racing? Did she think she was going to be beat or raped or murdered? Did she have children? Were they at home with her?

I could imagine what she was going through, what she was thinking. That fear racing through your blood. Feeling your heart beating so fast you think the world can hear it pounding against your chest walls. A light headedness takes over and you can't breathe, you are panting, quick, deep, shallow breaths, gasping for air. You are feeling as though the blood is draining right out of you because you are at that moment alone, there is no one to help you.

I know how this feels. One day in 1995, I went home on my lunch break from work. It was Christmas time and Sears was having a sale on Christmas decorations. I stopped home to see if I needed any new Christmas lights. When I opened the door to the L-shaped closet where they were stored, I leaned in about a foot. Through my peripheral vision I could see the silhouette of a man off to the right side, leaning up against the wall as tight as he could. He must have heard me coming and hid in the closet, fate would have it that I would open this door this day. I didn't dare turn my head in that direction. I knew what I was seeing and there was no need for any confirmation. I thought to get out of the house as fast as I could. I backed out and ran like hell.

I'm not sure why I ran to the phone in one of the rooms. I should have run straight to the door. Maybe because I could hear his footsteps pounding on the floor as he was coming after me, I thought if I got to the phone at least the police would know I was in trouble. I felt the adrenaline in my body surge through me. Shaking tremendously I managed to dial 911 as I could feel him coming up behind me. I was screaming into the phone, not sure if anyone was even there to hear me. I could feel him even closer and was ready to jump out through the window when I could feel his thick fingers on the back of my neck. His grip tight, I was screaming.. He reached from around my neck and grabbed my mouth to muffle me with one hand as he yanked the phone right out of my hand with his other. He pressed the "end" button on the phone and threw it across the room.

He turned me around and my fears had come true as I realized I knew who this person was. I was terrified. I don't remember what he was saying, but he was yelling at me. I bit his hand that held my face tightly and somehow managed to break away from his grip. Doubting the 911 call went through, I knew if I got outside I could probably outrun him. I needed to get outside regardless if I could outrun him or not. There was a world out there. There was nothing in here except the Devil's den, where I would have surely succumbed to evil.

I ran out the back door with him still coming after me. I ran around the backside of the house towards the long driveway that led to the street. When I came down and around I saw a police officer all ready getting out of his car at the bottom of the driveway. He started running up, talking into a radio at the same time, when he realized he was at the right place and I was in trouble. He could see clearly the fear in my face. As I was running for him he passed me yelling to me if I were okay. I couldn't speak, I just ran for his car. Another police car was approaching. My legs, only strong enough to take me to safety, collapsed, as I ran behind the first police car. I thought my heart was going to burst through my chest; I was gasping for air as I hid behind the tire of the car. I heard them yelling to him to get down. I managed to look back to make sure they had him. I saw him on the ground, his hands pinned behind his back and cuffed. I remember hoping the rocks on the driveway were cutting into his face pressed against the ground like his fingers had pressed and squeezed my neck and face.

My thoughts went back to the woman. Did she feel that immense fear that runs through your veins as easily as your blood flows? How could my son do this? What was he thinking when he entered her home? Apparently he wasn't thinking. He wasn't thinking of his future; he certainly wasn't thinking of her present.

My heart breaking, I wondered what had happened to him. He was out of my reach; he couldn't or wouldn't grab my hand for help. I felt like he was gone, like when we lose a loved one and we know in our heart that person is never coming back to us though our love would always be there. This just hurt so much more because he was not dead and yet I had absolutely no control over what he was doing with his life or how he was destroying it. I was powerless and I found myself mourning for my son's life, not his death.

Chapter Two

I cried and I cried and I cried. I cried by myself, I cried to my girlfriends, to my mother, searching for answers from them. My stomach was in knots. I couldn't eat and I couldn't sleep. I knew he had some issues but I never thought this would be Joey's life, sitting in jail because of a burglary charge.

I could only come up with one logical explanation as to why he would be in this position in the first place and it is a sad one. I blamed myself; I should have done more. I was responsible; I am his mother. I was not responsible; he is an adult. I went back and forth, back and forth. It was eating me up. I thought of everything that had led up to this. I should have seen it coming: his high school years, PINS petitions, reform schools, detention center. He was never "bad". I thought maybe oppositional and rebellious, but not a bad kid.

I thought Joey would have called me when he got to the jail but he did not. When the court opened on Monday I'm sure their phone was ringing off the hook, as I needed to know when Joey would be arraigned and what would happen after that. The man who answered the phone in the court office when I called was so wonderfully sympathetic. He understood that I lived upstate in Westchester and I was very concerned.

In spite of the fact that Joey was an adult now – as I am so frequently informed these days by law enforcement, peers, counselors- he was kind enough to let me know he was in Riverhead Correctional Facility, to call back tomorrow, on Tuesday, after Joey went in front of the judge, and that he would let me know if he was released or not.

I called the next day as he had said I should. He informed me that Joey was released and needed to return for an October court date. I asked him if my son would have been able to call me; he didn't see why he wouldn't be able to. I kindly thanked him and hung up the phone.

I wondered why my son hadn't called me. I wondered if he was purposefully not calling me as punishment because I didn't run out to Long Island.

Throughout the rest of the afternoon and evening my stomach continued to stay in knots. I was not going to leave the house in case he called. Every time the phone rang I jumped and was saddened that it was not him.

Finally, later in the evening, Joey had borrowed someone's cell phone to call, saying he was making his way back to the hotel where everyone was staying from his group in magazine sales. He filled me in on what the judge said. He told me he had no money, was starving, and didn't even know if he was walking in the right direction.

I felt helpless, battling emotions; I wanted to help him, but I wanted him to learn a lesson. I wanted to Western Union him some money, but I wanted him to know what feeling hungry felt like. I thought of somehow paying by telephone for him to take a cab to the hotel, but I wanted his feet to hurt from walking miles of shame. I was not going to give him any words of advice or hope. I wanted him to look deep inside himself for those answers. He was in a harsh, brutally cold world and I wanted him to realize it. I thought maybe this would be, could be, a huge wake up call for him. So, I simply just asked him to call me when he got back to the hotel so I would know he was safe.

After I hung the phone up, I felt good that I had heard his voice, but wondered if he was manipulating me. Why I let him do this to me, I thought. He was not that scared or that hungry, because if he was, he would have called his dad, my mother, the boy's father, an uncle, a friend, or any number of people to reach out to for help if he felt I could not help him.

I was scared for him. I was sad, angry, disappointed, frustrated...and the list just went on, as did this emotional rollercoaster ride. I never thought it was possible to feel so many emotions in one frame of time, broken down into a fragment of seconds that wreaks havoc in your heart. It seemed as though it had been going on for years. It had been going on for years. When was it going to stop?

Grief is a word that encompasses all the emotions I had in regards to my relationship with my son. I was grieving the loss of a once funny, artistic, athletic child, a young man whose intelligence was remarkable. What happened to my baby? Why was he angry and resentful?

Unbeknownst to the two younger boys, I had somehow managed to maintain a sense of calmness in the home. I had managed to be discreet and keep this private from them. It's amazing how strong a mother can be in front of her children when she needs to be when in reality she is bursting at the seams with heartache that would make tears so big they flow into their own river of sadness.

After hanging up from our short conversation, sunset had come and gone and the darkness that fell over the earth was only lit by moonlight. I began to wonder how many long dark nights I would be in for.

I realized I would have no idea where Joey was unless he called me. I wouldn't know if he was eating, or in a bed safe at night. I would have no idea if he felt desperate enough to steal again. I suddenly remembered he had taken the job with his friend Owen, whose life was also going nowhere fast. They had been friends for many years and I was sure he would look out for him, at least until he got paid.

I never liked Owen; he could never look me in the eye. I remembered the day I was driving up the block he happened to live on, he never saw me coming, and as I approached I couldn't believe my eyes. He was making a drug deal right at the bottom of the steps that led up to his mother's home. It was right in the middle of the day and I felt like pulling over and knocking on her door and telling her. Unfortunately, I realized that she had to have already known and turned a blind eye, as many mothers do, as she had another son, who had no job but drove a BMW. I guess it never occurred to her where he would get money to buy a luxury car.

As I passed by, I beeped. When he saw me he gave me a strange look; guilt that he had been caught doing something wrong. I looked back at him with a look that must have confirmed that.

When I brought it to Joey's attention, he, of course, denied that Owen sold drugs and said I must have seen someone that looked like him. I couldn't believe he insulted my intelligence but understood that they had been best friends since childhood so naturally he would not admit it. I simply told him I knew exactly who and what I saw and told him Owen was never to be in my house again.

As parents, I think we tend to blame our children's friends for their failures and/or their negative outcomes. I use to think Owen was a bad influence on Joey. I wonder now if it could've been Joey who was a bad influence on Owen.

The next day, Joey was kind enough to call me from the hotel. He said he spoke with his manager and somehow finagled him in to letting him keep his job. I told him that that was good, to keep his head up, to stay out of trouble, and all the other motherly things we tell our children.

After that conversation, I hadn't heard from him in days. The weekend had arrived and I still hadn't heard from him. I left messages with management, but he wouldn't return any of my calls.

I had lost about ten or twelve pounds, I had bags under my eyes, and apparently it was starting to affect me at work. My boss, Fred had taken me outside and practically tore my head off for something I did. I knew that if it was affecting me here it was affecting me everywhere and I wasn't seeing it, being I am not the type of person to take my problems or my tears to work. I apologized sincerely, taking full responsibility, and knew I had to get it together.

It was Wednesday the following week when I was driving through town and thought I saw Owen. I even took a double-take but blew it off that maybe it must have been his brother since Owen was on Long Island.

The next day after work I was going to drop my other boys off at their dad's after I picked them up from school but I first needed to run home to grab something.

There was a visitor inside waiting for us. "Hi, Mom," as if all was well, I heard Joey say. I was speechless. I couldn't believe he had the audacity to stand there after not contacting me for well over a week. I was in shock. I instantaneously felt a surge of anger rush through me.

Before he took the job on Long Island I had asked him to leave my home for good. I was tired of his lies, his stealing from me and his brothers, the nasty comments he would make to us and the provocation of arguments between him and me, or worse him and his brothers.

I knew my son and I knew he was going to manipulate this. I knew he thought because a few weeks had gone by, that he could just move back in without any recourse. I told the boys to hurry and told Joey I would speak with him later when I got back.

Adam, my other boys' father who was not Joey's dad, lived only a few moments away. As I was taking the boys there, I heard them talking in the car. I don't remember what they were talking about. I couldn't hear or speak; it was as if I had suddenly become mute. I felt anxiety creeping up. How was I going to handle this? If I only had a little bit of time to prepare. But to be caught off guard, I felt a crash of emotions like bumper cars banging into each other within my own heart, crucifying me and the choices I made as a mother no matter which direction I took, no matter which decision I would make.

And as that mother I was relieved to know he was physically safe and that he seemed okay. But he was not okay, I was not okay. This behavior was insane. The feelings went to anger. How dare he just show up! The selfishness he showed in not keeping in touch with anyone was nothing but rude and disrespectful. He showed absolutely no regard for anyone. My mother, who adores him, called everyday to see if I had heard something from him, and every day I would tell her "no."

I felt sick, physically sick, and my nerves were just rumbling. I dropped the boys off and didn't even say" I love you" to them, as I always do before we depart. They walked into the house and I drove off. I went back home. When I pulled into my own driveway, I just sat in the car for a few moments. I needed to pray for guidance and get my thoughts together. I knew I needed to be firm. This was going to rip me apart, but I knew I had to hold my ground. If I kept giving in to his lies and manipulation nothing would change. I would only be enabling him to continue his negative lifestyle. I wanted to believe badly that every time he said he was going to change, he truly meant it. But, sadly, that was never the case.

I was the mother. If I didn't change, how would he have any chance at changing? I was the mother. I needed to stop this cycle. I was the mother. I didn't want to lose my son to prison, drugs, or death, and that was the path he was on. I might not be able to change him but I could change how I reacted to him, which might inadvertently change the direction of his behavior.

Chapter Three

I took a deep breath as I entered through the front door. Joey was in the kitchen. I looked him in the face and sternly said, "You cannot stay here. I'm sorry but I can't go through this anymore. It hasn't been only one or two incidences, Joey. It's been dozens over and over again. You've lied, you've stolen, you've manipulated, you've abused. I just can't do it anymore."

"But mom please," he cried. "Where am I going to go? I have nowhere to go, Mom. Please give me another chance." He begged me with his eyes filling with tears, surely not expecting this from me.

"Listen to me," I said to him. "When you came back here to live five months ago, I only let you come back under the pretense that you were entering the United States Army. What happened to that, Joey? You went upstate for over a month so you could get clean and be able to pass the drug test to get in. You came back here and didn't last three days before you started hanging with your old crew and getting high again. I knew in my heart it would only be a matter of time before all this started up again. You have a serious problem."

"Mom, you make it sound like I'm an addict. I'm no addict!" He screamed at me.

I maintained calmness in my voice because if I reacted to his screaming I knew I would lose control over this situation; it would turn ugly, and who knew if something would get broken, or maybe another hole in the wall, because he couldn't control his anger. "When I told you, you had to leave over a month ago the reason was why, Joey? You had stolen from me and your brothers yet again. Not to mention that you brought drugs into my home. Is your memory coming back yet? How much can I take? I found a pouch with a white powdery residue. Do you remember my bringing that to your attention? How dare you bring drugs into my home where your brothers sleep! You brought cocaine here…"

I was interrupted at this point by him now screaming at me, "It wasn't cocaine, all right! It was fucking crack! Okay?"

I was speechless. He said it as though crack wasn't as bad as cocaine, as if I could be upset but it wasn't the end of the world so get over it already. I stood there looking at him trying to process what I had just heard. Did he just finally admit something to me? It was one of those deaf mute moments again. He was standing there looking back at me. I wasn't sure if he was realizing what he said. Maybe he didn't mean to be that straightforward with me, but it was too late; it was out there.

"Go," I finally was able to say softly, "just go." He didn't say anything. He just started walking towards the door. When he opened it, I called his name and in a quiet, calm, but very firm tone said, "Don't come back." He looked back at me with a blank stare in his eyes and walked out, leaving the door wide open behind him.

I walked over to shut the door then I looked on the wall behind me. There hung three separate black-and-white headshots of the boys in the entryway. I wanted to see each of their beautiful faces when I walked in or out the front door. I wanted whom ever came to my door to see their beautiful faces. My eyes met Joey's photo. It was a picture of him with the Atlantic Ocean in the background; he was looking out towards it. The picture was taken a few years ago. I believe it was the last time he went away with us. It was actually around the time our family started to fall apart. With that thought, I fell to my hands and knees sobbing.

I cried so hard so fast that I was starting to hyperventilate. I cried until I couldn't cry anymore. My head hurt so badly from crying, I felt like it was going to explode from the pressure if one more tear escaped me. It was as though someone had died. I suppose in essence someone had...my child's spirit. My child has evolved into a different person. That sweet little boy, that humorous young man was gone, his spirit dead.

Crack, I thought. I couldn't believe it. I asked myself how I could not know. Crack...was my son using, selling, both? After the tears stopped and my breathing slowly returned to normal, I continued to lie on the cold ceramic tile staring up at the small cobweb in the corner of the ceiling looking at the tiny fly that was trapped and couldn't get out. I thought that life had transitioned. It was no longer how I knew it to be. Nor did I believe that it would ever return to how it was.

I realized it is not just my son...it is your son and your sister's son; it is your neighbor's daughter and your boss's child. There is a whole society of young adults who have become lost souls. Why are we losing our children? It seems the world has gone crazy as though it is drunk off the alcohol-induced oceans it lays upon and whose waves are coming up and swallowing our children in huge ferocious gulps.

I prayed to God again. I couldn't recall how many times in the past few weeks I had prayed to him. I'd been talking to God in the car, in the shower, while cooking, cleaning, at the drive-thru at the bank, while on the phone waiting for the other end to be answered.

I prayed while I was lying on the cold hard floor crying. "Oh, dear Lord, you must be tired of me by now. I wish Joey could find you in his heart. You have your own miraculous way of showing yourself to people to let them know you are there for them. I pray you send an angel to my child to show him there is some light in his future, that he will embrace you in his heart, accept you and know through you he has the power to change his life, because I cannot."

I have to pick myself up off this floor, I thought. My body seemed to find comfort on it. It was a hot August evening and the coldness from the floor brought relief to me.   I had decided to stay for just a few more minutes. As I looked up at the spider web, I wondered if that fly knew his life would forever be altered the moment he entered the web.

I needed to come up with a plan to save this child of mine so now that he was caught in a web maybe his life wouldn't have to be altered, there are some, few, but some flies that do manage to escape the web of addiction.

Chapter Four

It was so quiet at home since I had last seen saw Joey and told him he couldn't stay here. The boys asked about him and I was very honest with them, not necessarily believing they needed to know everything, but under the circumstances they were living this with me so it was only fair of me to help them understand.

I sat the boys down to explain to them that Joey would not be staying with us. My youngest son broke out crying. He had an ideal notion of how and what a family should be. He wanted all of us to be able to be united. He wanted all of us to get along and love each other unconditionally. He had an immense sweetness about him that we all should carry in our hearts.

My words were piercing to him as I explained Joey's behavior. As his young mind absorbed every aching word I spoke, he realized I was very serious about not letting Joey back in the house. In spite of all the pain and all the drama he had caused this family over literally years, his baby brother still wanted him here with us. He sat there and listened to me, and then he cried. He cried because he felt that loss of a brother as I had been feeling of a son.

My middle son, however, was sadly quite relieved. He was quiet as he intently listened to me. When I finished, he asked me if I meant it this time. I could tell he was very concerned that I might not, being that I had allowed Joey back in the home before. He was a bit older than the younger one and had different experiences with Joey that the younger one really wasn't aware of.

He would forever remember the last day he ever wanted anything to do with his big brother. He had always been the object of Joey's anger and put up with abuse in different forms from him for much longer than he cared to. The last day will forever be etched in his mind with not-so-fondest memories. I was sure the past five months, in retrospect, had been very difficult for him. I know they had been for me.

That day had been building up. The same things had been going on. But what was worse than the getting high and stealing was the lack of respect he showed for this family. Little things would just set Joey off. One day we went to Motor Vehicle for him to get his driving permit.

There was a misunderstanding about a paper he needed. It was something so simple that could have been taken care of in a day but, instead of listening, he lost it; he cursed out the lady that worked there and stormed out. Besides being angry, I was mortified. I didn't know what else I could do except apologize to the lady. My mother was with us and she was just quiet, though I could hear her whispering softly the words "My God" under her breath. The lady looked at me with sadness in her eyes, not insult, not anger, not hatred, just sadness. She knew I had trouble on my hands. She was the one who was sorry for me.

As I walked out, I felt all eyes on me, looking at me as though I had the most disrespectful, ungrateful teenager on this earth. And at that moment I can't say I would've disagreed.

That following Sunday was cold but beautiful, and on Sundays I would get to make the boys a big, yummy breakfast; a day we would usually enjoy. I was upstairs straightening up the bedrooms. I was in mine when Anthony came in with a not-so-happy look on his face. He kept saying nothing was wrong but his face said something else. I even pretty much knew without him telling me that Joey had probably said or did something to him, most likely trying to provoke him into an argument. Sometimes I do believe it's not really to argue with Anthony but to lure me into an argument, because he knows if he starts with Anthony I will protect him.

Joey enjoys arguing as much as some people enjoy dancing. I suppose you could say the tango is Joey's favorite dance since it takes two to do so. My brain was already in motion thinking how not to entertain his offer for a dance.

Anthony and I were talking when Joey came in the room and asked me for some money. I told him no. I told him no because he had lost three jobs due to his attitude. Anthony was sitting on my bed looking at the floor, not wanting to make eye contact with him. Joey walked out. Joey walked back in and asked me for money. Again, I said no. This went on for a few minutes. I knew what was coming. I had to dance even though I didn't want to. There was no way of avoiding it. I could feel the tension rising. I could see the anger and uneasiness taking residence in his face. The sheet music never changes. I could just about hear the music start to play. We were almost there. We were walking to the dance floor, getting ready to dance. Joey entered the room, "Mom, can I have some money, please?" He asked me in a demanding tone that said I'd better give him some money or there was going to be a problem. I could not give in to his-off- to-the-side way of threats. I told him I didn't have any money, this was relentless badgering, and I was not going to give in to it.

Now even Anthony was at this point tired of the same old beat. He was tired of his repetitive asking and he was tired of having to repeatedly go through this. Calmly, Anthony said, "Mommy said she doesn't have any. Why do you keep asking her?"

It happened so fast. He stood still for just a moment in the doorway looking at Anthony. His face was blank but his eyes raged with hatred as if the devil himself had come to teach him how to dance.

He snapped. He lunged across the room toward Anthony, tackling him, his large body completely covering Anthony's. I started to scream. I could see his hand coming up and being drawn back with a cocked fist. My eyes watched in slow motion as his fist pummeled down with force into Anthony's ribs. I couldn't get across the room fast enough. I heard Anthony cry out in pain as I lunged onto Joey's back. His fist erupted into an explosion of punches. I grabbed the back of his shirt to pull him off of Anthony. His fist was getting ready to make contact again when I could hear A.J. screaming and crying behind me. Over my screams I could hear him talking to someone. Thankfully I knew he had called 911. Anthony was screaming to me, "Mommy, get him off! I can't breathe! Mommy, help me! I can't breathe!" as Joey's fist came thrashing down again into his side.

At that moment he was no longer my child; he was a man who was attacking my child. With all the strength I had, I started hitting him and pulling on him to get him off of Anthony. I finally somehow managed to throw my body in between him and Anthony. He was ready to hit me when he realized A.J. was on the phone with the police, and he ran out of the house. I ran to shut my bedroom door and lock it when I heard him swearing and cursing how much he hated me on his way out.

I took the phone from A.J. who was crying and hugging his brother. My hand was trembling. As I said I needed help, the officer could hear the fear in my voice. "Sheila, I have cars on the way. Are you okay?" I broke down crying as I recognized the familiar voice that had been to my home so many times in the past to help resolve issues with Joey's erratic behavior.

He was trying to ask me what happened as the boys started screaming when they thought Joey was coming back in the house, but the noise they heard was, thankfully, the police.

The agonizing fact was that this was their brother, my son, who caused this heart-wrenching event in our lives. Anthony's pain ran deeper than the blows to his ribcage; it ran straight to his heart. His relationship with Joey would forever be changed, altered by emotional scars that would run just too deep to ever heal completely.

This had escalated to another level that could not be tolerated. I think I always knew in my heart that he was capable of crossing over the line into violence. There had been many things smashed, thrown and broken in this house over the past few years. Many holes put in the walls, I suppose, to avoid hitting the person who his anger was directed at, that being his brother or myself. I guess it was only a matter of time before he struck out at someone in this family.

He was out of the house now, for two reasons; Anthony and A.J. I knew, reflecting on this event and past events that I needed to be strong and hold my ground. I needed to let him go this time for good. I prayed that I would be strong enough. Nothing would ever change if I was not strong.

Somehow we needed to find our way to a normal healthy environment where we could function as a somewhat normal family. It was up to me to lead my sons on that path.

Chapter Five

I hadn't slept well since even before Joey left. Now it was even worse. I woke up all throughout the night. I had only heard from him once since that awful day, and the conversation was brief; I suppose it was only for him to try and break the ice with me. I believe he was trying to feel me out, to see where I was standing emotionally with him, to see if I were going to give in and tell him how much I was worried about him.

About almost two weeks had passed, I was mentally exhausted, and finally one night I fell asleep the moment my body hit the mattress. It was one of those good sleeps where you feel you are a part of the mattress, your body molds into it and takes form in it.

When I woke up, the clock read 3:30 a.m. I was just staring at the bright light on the clock thinking, if I just close my eyes I will drift back to where I was. It felt as though I had been asleep for days. So unfortunate to realize it had only been a few hours. It's amazing how our bodies are affected when we worry about our children. I thought if I could just keep a relaxed, peaceful feeling I might be able to fall back to sleep. I thought of yoga movements, I relaxed my mind, then my neck, my shoulders, my back. It was working. I could feel my body sinking peacefully back into the mattress. I was thankful that finally I was going to get a good night's rest.

Suddenly, I was jolted awake with fear of an unknown sound. My eyes opened wide. I lay there frozen, trying to figure out where it was coming from. Maybe one of the boys had gotten up to go to the bathroom. I got up out of bed, grabbed the phone instinctively, and started to walk down the hall towards their bedrooms. As I got closer and looked in, I saw they were both asleep. I heard it again but couldn't place what kind of sound it was. My heart was quickly racing as a familiar sense of panic kicked in.

I crept into Anthony's room to look out the window that was halfway opened because there was a nice Indian summer breeze flowing through. I knew I had to be extremely quiet since the window was open. I heard the noise again. It was a tinkering noise against the outside of the house. I got close to the window and was able to gently pull the curtain slightly so I could peek out. I could see the shadow of a man. I let the curtain close and with that, I must have been seen or heard, as there was a knock on the front door.

I sat down on the edge of Anthony's bed thinking of what to do, because I knew it was Joey. A small rock he threw through the window hit me on my shoulder. I assumed he was trying to wake Anthony up to let him in. I sat there and watched little rocks entering the room and landing on the floor. Some would miss and hit the metal that framed the windows outside and some would hit the glass making a clicking sound. I didn't want any drama tonight. I didn't want to let Joey in because I knew that if I did, nothing would be learned except accepting the fact that I was an enabler.

I couldn't think quickly enough how to handle this situation. In between knocking, he was throwing rocks, and they were getting louder and faster. I knew he wasn't going to go away. I heard some banging and clanking and quickly realized there was a shed about three feet from Anthony's window. He must have been trying to climb and was going to jump to the window when he got on top of it.

I knew I had a problem, so I took a deep breath and walked over to the window. He was standing on top of the shed.

"Joey, what are you doing?"

"Mom, I have no place to stay."

I looked down at Anthony sleeping and realized I couldn't do this to him. He needed to feel safe. I knew that if I let Joey in, the drama would continue, and I had to hold my ground for all of our sakes.

I made a very difficult decision and told him he needed to go back to wherever he was coming from at this hour. He was telling me over and over how he would do the right thing if I let him back in. He appeared drunk to me, as he was trying to climb back down off the shed. He was sweating profusely. I can't count the times I have heard him say, "if only I did this," or "if only I did that" he would straighten up. I told him I was sorry but I couldn't let him in and that if he went to rehab and got the proper help he needed then we could discuss his returning to our home. I felt that was the right thing to say because it left him with an option and an option that he would be responsible for.

He didn't seem right to me and I had an eerie feeling about this scenario and how it would play out. I was thinking about the time I was cleaning his room and came across a Magic Marker, I came across another one as I was empting his pockets for laundry, and another one was in another pocket. I decided to look around, not sure why I was doing what I was doing, but something didn't feel right to me. I looked on shelves, in drawers, under the bed, and in the closet. I found sixteen black Magic Markers. I decided to call a dear friend of mine, Andrew, who was a police officer and also worked in a drug court. I had heard somewhere that people get high off of smelling markers so I asked him if it were true that people could get high off of them. His response was, "Of course, Sheila. It's a cheap high. It's called huffing."

I was explaining to Joey he had a very serious problem and needed an intense treatment program. He told me he would do out-patient. I told him sniffing paint and smelling Magic Markers and whatever else he was indulging in were not things I felt could be treated on an out-patient basis. He denied getting high this way but he denied a lot of things. I also explained to him that I felt he could benefit from some counseling and anger management programs.

He started to pace, and I knew with his actions this was going to escalate. I felt from all of our past experiences this would not be good; I felt very nervous and quickly called 911 and held the phone behind the curtain to speak so he couldn't see me if he looked up at the window. I talked low and fast. Joey was saying something, but I couldn't quite understand what it was. He started knocking harder on the door, insisting I let him in. I was sure my neighbors were up by now. I was also thinking I did the right thing by making that call. Then he started banging on the door even harder. I told him I had called the police and he should leave before things get worse. He screamed at me, "I'm not going anywhere!" He screamed at me, "You're going to need the police to get rid of me!"

Oh, my God, I thought. I pointed out that only a few moments ago he was saying he wouldn't give me any more problems and he would go to a treatment program.

How fast promises go out the window when we don't get our way, or really what we need. In his case to get in here for whatever his reasons would be, so, hence, he would have his most expectant meltdown since I would not allow him in the home.

This I knew was not going to be good. His anger and lack of control seemed to definitely be escalating. Anthony was moving around in his bed and I was praying that he would not wake up right now.

One police car, two police cars, three police cars, and three more came behind those. A couple of the officers knew him by his first name, of course. I heard them saying, "Hey, Joey, what's going on?" Another officer was knocking on my front door, so I closed Anthony's window and went downstairs to talk to him. He wanted to ask me a few questions about what happened. I explained to him what had happened two weeks ago and why I was not letting him in, so he told me they would tell him he would have to leave. He also said that if I had any more problems, to call them.

I could hear Joey yelling at them in the background that he wasn't going anywhere. The officer went outside to see why Joey was acting this way. I locked the door and went upstairs to sit on my bed to pray. As I was praying for my family, my son, his addiction, his anger, his depression, his heartache, I heard a loud, strange "pop". I froze for a second, trying to process what I had heard. I ran down the hall back to Anthony's room. As I was running to his window, Anthony was up, also in motion towards his window, asking me what was going on, asking me what that noise was. I couldn't answer him.

I looked out the window and saw the police cars but no police. I could hear panic in Anthony's voice as he asked me again what was happening and why there were half a dozen police cars outside the house. I knew he was thinking the same thing I was. I could hear yelling from around the block. I told him to stay inside. I ran out of his room, down the hall to the stairs, I sped down the stairs and out the front door into the darkness.

As I leapt into the front yard, my neighbor was standing in her front yard. I ran down the path, and as I was running toward the sound, the sergeant was running back to his car. I could see sweat glistening on his face from the reflection of the moonlight. I asked him what the "pop" was a few moments earlier but he didn't respond to me. I asked him again louder. He responded with an angry tone of voice, "Your son! If I were you, I would go get paper."

What the hell does that mean, I thought? I heard a soft voice asking me if I was okay. I couldn't answer her because I couldn't see my son and didn't know what that "pop" sound was.

My brain was scrambling to make sense of each sound and movement the officers were making to draw my own conclusions. I thought if it were a gunshot he would not have answered me with the response he did. He got in his car and sped off.

Three of the officers were walking back towards their cars. I asked them what the loud popping noise I heard was and "Where is Joey?" They told me Joey had run on them but turned and threw a large rock which had hit the "Stop" sign. I sat down on the steps and exhaled. Thank God, I thought. My mind had envisioned Joey grabbing one of their guns and turning it on them or one of the officers firing their gun at him for some unknown reason.

Joey was arrested for disorderly conduct and resisting arrest. They told me to go to the station tomorrow for papers for an order of protection. I immediately realized that that's what the sergeant had meant when he said I should get papers. I wondered if it was to the level I actually needed an order of protection from my own child. From the sergeant's perspective, it apparently was. One of the officers asked me whether I knew if my son used PCP, otherwise known as "dust." I had no idea. He explained to me that that behavior was in line with someone who uses it.

As I walked back up the path to my townhouse numb, exhausted and confused I happened to look up at Anthony's bedroom window. He had been so quiet leaning into it the whole time watching and listening. I stopped for a moment and we just looked at each other. The sadness in his face was also highlighted by the reflection of the moon. I pierced my lips together as if to give a look that said maybe one of these days it would be okay. He looked back at me with eyes of uncertainty and disbelief. This poor kid just kept witnessing and being affected by this insane, horrendous behavior of his big brother. When would it stop?

I went inside and made my way upstairs to A.J.'s room. He, thankfully, had slept through the whole ordeal. I went into Anthony's room and crawled into bed with him. I hugged him tightly and told him how much I loved him.

"Promise me Anthony you will never do drugs."

"I promise Mommy," he whispered back.

I held him until he fell asleep and then I walked down the dark hallway to my bedroom. As I lay down looking again at the green neon light on the clock, which now read nearly 5:00 a.m., I wondered at which moment in time it was in Joey's life that I had lost him.

Chapter Six

The moonlight faded off the tips of the tree branches as the morning sun tried to shine through the crack of the drapes that hung from my bedroom windows. I didn't sleep the rest of the night, or maybe I should say early morning. I stared out the window to see the transition of the new day arriving. I could only think of Joey, the burglary charges that were hanging over his head, as well as now these new charges of resisting arrest and disorderly conduct. I could only think of how his life was on this downward cycle spiraling out of control.

I never intended for him to be arrested; I just wanted him to leave. I just wanted a little peace. I was so tired of having to go through all this drama and heartache over and over again. I was tired of the boys being subject to the emotional torture of not knowing at what given moment their brother was going to explode and make them feel unsafe. Worse, I felt as though there would be a moment or day that I could not protect them from his rages and outbursts.

I called the police station later that day to see if he was remanded by the Court or not. They informed me he had been arraigned by the judge for his behavior the night before and released. The judge decided to let him go and told him he would have to return to court on another date. The judge did, however, issue an order of protection for us, which was delivered to me later that evening. The order of protection stated that he was not allowed near the home, not allowed to call the home or my job. Basically, he wasn't allowed to be around me or the boys.

It was a very profound moment in my life. The police handed me this piece of paper and it was indescribable. This child came from the fibers of my body and I was being given an order of protection against my own child. His blood was my blood and with each broken heartbeat I wish he could have felt how my heart hurt and bled for his well-being. His ears were my ears. Why couldn't he hear the words I said to him? His eyes were my eyes. I wish he could see how I saw with them so he could see what he was doing with his life. Now by his behavior and an order of the State of N.Y. he was not allowed any contact with the woman who bore him life.

I knew as much as it hurt, that at this moment in time it was for the best. I hoped that this would shake him up a bit. I wondered if it had an impact on him when he had to sign the order of protection in court. How could it not be a defining moment in anyone's life? You were being told by a judge that you couldn't have any contact with your mother or family. That thought alone has to be beyond one of immense sadness.

Almost twenty-one years ago I gave birth to this beautiful baby that I promised I would love and protect for his entire life, and no matter what he did in his life, good or bad, right or wrong. I would always be there and love him unconditionally.

I went back to the very beginning and thought of all the choices I had made from the time I found out I was pregnant and the early years of his childhood. I questioned a few decisions I had made and I felt that I needed to take some responsibility and accept the fact that somewhere along the road I had dropped the ball on this kid.

The thoughts I was having led me to his father, Travis. I had just graduated from high school and I traveled back to London, where I fully anticipated moving permanently to so that I could be closer to my family. When I had come back to the states to do my paperwork and visit my mother, I was introduced to Travis through a friend of mine who knew his cousin. He told me he was twenty-four. We started dating and I found out later he was actually pushing thirty.

He was kind, always thinking of other people, he spoiled me completely, and we had a lot fun together. I was not of a legal age to drink, so I couldn't get into any clubs or hotspots in the City, so we did other things, like concerts, amusement parks, movies and dinner. While we dated, I prolonged going back to London, and after a few months I missed my period.

My God, what would my Irish-Catholic mother say? I knew I would be a huge disappointment to her because I wasn't married and she had always told me growing up that I should wait until I was married to have sexual relations with a man. Then I thought of my stepfather, who I was sure this would have stressed out simply because my mother would be upset, disappointed, and embarrassed. My somewhat-at-times-rebellious self of course found some humor in seeing the look on his face when the news was told. I needed to figure out how I was going to tell them that their teenage, unmarried, catholic daughter was having their illegitimate grandchild by a man nearly thirty years old.

Three months passed. I had moved out of my parents' home without their finding out that I was pregnant. Things were still going nicely with Travis. One night as we were food shopping and were putting groceries in the car, something fell out of his sweatshirt pocket. He very quickly covered it with his feet. He was looking at me with a strange look on his face and suddenly seemed nervous. I asked him what it was and he didn't answer. I remember looking down at his large sneakers as they covered the mysterious object. He had a slight smile on his face, a nervous smile. He finally bent down without moving his feet, trying to pick it up without my seeing what it was. I asked him again what it was. Without saying a word, he held his hand out and opened it up so I could see.

I just stared at it. I couldn't believe my eyes. I was in utter shock. A thousand thoughts raced through my brain. I thought of my mother, my family, my friends, my life, my dreams, the future, my unborn baby's future. Did I want to now be with this man the rest of my life? I looked back up at him. I don't remember what words were exchanged, if any, since I think I suddenly became foggy-headed. I looked back down into his hand. Inside I could feel my eyes begin to tear. I enjoyed him, I appreciated him, but I didn't love him, and when I found out I was pregnant I thought perhaps maybe one day I would.

Just staring into his hand looking at it with such disbelief, I thought of how he told me he worked in construction, that was a lie, I felt betrayed. I felt sick. I asked myself how naïve could I possibly have been?

There in his hand was a small plastic bag with little pieces of what looked like small chunks of soap. Travis asked me if I knew what it was and I nodded my head yes. I knew what it was because I had a friend whose boyfriend sold it and she showed it to me one day behind his back. He asked me if I was okay, but I really just wanted to not have that conversation in the parking lot of a shopping center. As we drove home to my apartment it was quiet and I felt inside of me that whatever hope I had of doing what was right and trying to make a family with this man had just instantaneously left my soul. I had serious thinking to do and I had a very serious decision to make.

Chapter Seven

The phone rang. It was my mother. I thought she was calling to ask me if I were going to watch the ceremonies regarding the anniversary of 9/11. I couldn't believe it had been seven years since that awful day in our nation's history. Unfortunately, my mother was calling to inform me that she spoke with Joey and that he didn't sound good. I asked her what she meant, though I think I already knew. She explained that she thought he was suicidal. In an instant I had thought of all the times over the past few years he had said to me in the midst of his tantrums that he never should have been born or why did I have him. I actually had a crisis team at my house on one occasion when he was a teenager because he said he wanted to die. So now I went into panic mode not knowing if he was just threatening it or actually meant it.

When I was younger I had a boyfriend who attempted suicide and it was so very ugly. I will never forget seeing him in the ER, his face pale, ashen, his eyes sunken with dark rings under them, and his mouth and chin dipped in what looked like black tar. It was something the doctors had used to pump his stomach with. As his eyes met mine they reflected fear and regret, his poor mother shaken with disbelief to the absolutely bone chilling reality that death was creeping invitingly into this young man's world by his own choice.

So, when my son threatened, I panicked. I wasn't aware at that time that some people use threats of suicide as a method of fierce manipulation. I wasn't a psychiatrist, so who was I to decipher who was and was not going to follow through with threats of taking their own life? My boyfriend at the time, who was ironically at the age Joey was now, never threatened that he would try to do such a thing; he just did it.

Though reflecting back, I was still focused on the conversation with my mother. I wasn't quite sure which friend Joey was staying with, but I knew it would most likely be one out of three kids. I told her I would look for him and try to talk to him.

Shortly after I got off the phone with my mother, the phone rang again but the number that was on the Caller ID was that of Joey's friend Lou. Common sense told me it was Joey calling, not Lou, and I was right. I thought that obviously he didn't care about the order of protection.

Of course, I didn't have to answer the phone, but after the conversation I just had with my mother, how could I not?

I said hello as if I didn't know it was him. He immediately said, "Hey, Ma, I know I'm not supposed to be calling you. I won't anymore after this." There was a pause. "You're just going to see Ma."

"I'm going to see what, Joey?"

"You're going to see real soon. Everyone is going to see." He hung up the phone.

I held onto the phone, wondering what he meant. I thought of the conversation with my mother and his strange behavior lately. I wondered if he meant he was going to hurt me or himself. I realized he really was not in a healthy mindset or a good place. Concerned, I went to the police department to file a report. I thought it would be a wise idea not necessarily to protect myself from him but maybe to protect him from himself.

The next morning I was driving A.J. to school. It was an on-and-off rainy kind of Friday morning. My cell phone rang and it was my mother. Her voice was not the same. She was trying to remain non-alarming as she proceeded to tell me that Joey had called her. He told her this was the day he was going to do it.

Each follicle of hair stood up on me, as I knew exactly what she meant. A feeling of dread, fright, anxiety, and extreme fear as I never knew it before took over me. I continued to listen as my mother went on to tell me the details of their conversation of how he was tired of living this way. I could feel my heart beating quicker. Then she told me piercing words that cut through my soul. She told me he told her how he planned to do it. He said he would take pills and alcohol so he would just go to sleep and it would be over. "Oh, my God!" I cried out loud.

I needed to get off the phone. "Mom, I have to call the police right now! I will call you back."

I could hear her voice choking back the tears as she calmly said, "Okay, Sheila."

Only a few blocks to the school, I picked up speed. I was calling for God to help me. I was demanding that He helped me. The tears were coming out now, flooding my eyes. I would not be able to live if my son took his life. My breathing was getting more difficult; I could feel my chest tightening up. I was already blaming myself; "Please, God, do not let Joey go through with this. Oh, my God, please."

Amazingly at that moment a female police officer came around the corner. The minute she saw me she knew something was wrong. She pulled her car over and as I managed to pull mine over I jumped out hysterically, trying to explain the situation to her. She was calm as she asked me if I thought he was serious and suddenly I was also calm as I heartbreakingly realized this was not manipulation. I could suddenly feel his pain and I couldn't take it away. I wanted to collapse on the street. And as the water filled the edge of my eyes and one tear at a time dropped over, I answered her in a soft voice, "Yes; yes; I do."

We agreed that I would meet her at the station in a few minutes, after I dropped A.J. off at school. When I got there we had to determine where Joey was. I remembered the number on the Caller ID. For some reason it could not be traced to an address, but I knew which apartment complex Lou lived in from dropping Joey off one time; I just didn't know which apartment it was. I was pretty sure this is where he was still at, so we decided to go up there after the sergeant agreed, and another male officer met us there.

Lou's girlfriend's car, thankfully, was in the parking lot, which meant the police were able to run the license plate to get the exact address. I knew time was ticking and I had no clue what state Joey was in. When the information came back, it was crushing, they told me it was registered to an old address where she used to live and that she had not changed it.

I waited anxiously by my car while the police decided to go knock on every door in the rain. The seconds turned into minutes and the minutes seemed endless until they did finally find him.

They spoke with him, then came back and told me he seemed fine.

"What?" I couldn't believe what I was hearing. In order for them to take him into custody or have a crisis team take him in for even an evaluation he would need to give them a reason to believe he was mentally or emotionally unstable. He was not a minor, so their hands were tied. They told me he denied saying any of the things my mother had told me. They told me he was upset that he wasn't working but did have interviews lined up and there was nothing they could legally do under the circumstances.

I was absolutely dumbfounded. I was helpless. This kid is crying, screaming, for help. I felt as though I was in a state of complex peril. I did not have a good feeling and ran deep through me.

They sincerely apologized for not being able to do anything. They knew what I told them was true. They knew and believed that this could have a God-awful ending. They told me to call them if anything else happened. They shook my hand and walked away. I cried as I walked to my car in the rain.

I sat in my car crying. I drove to work feeling probably the lowest I've ever felt in my life. The fear was immense and kept me trapped in a daze. I tried to keep busy at work. I tried to talk to my girlfriends; maybe they could give me advice, support. I didn't know what I needed, but I knew I needed something. I needed my son to be healthy and functioning, I needed my son back, and no one could give me that - not even my son.

The day was going to go on and that meant that the night was going to come. I was fearful of the approaching evening. I could feel all day in my heart, in the pit of my stomach that Joey meant every word he had said to my mother.

Though life can have obstacles, it is beautiful, and I couldn't understand what was so bad in life that someone would consider ending theirs. Why especially can't young people see they have their whole life ahead of them? What puts someone in such a state that they don't care about their future or care about the loved ones they will leave behind? Drugs do. Drugs are destroying families, destroying our youth... destroying my son.

In heavy thought, all of a sudden it hit me, Joey had called me. I called a friend of mine in the police dept. who was aware of what was going on with my son and genuinely cared. We became friends through the years of Joey growing up and all the turmoil. I told him where he was and that he violated the order of protection by calling me. I wanted him to be arrested (for his own safety). I also informed him about the pills and alcohol conversation he had with my mother earlier that morning.

He was great. He was able to obtain a court order on the grounds that Joey violated the order of protection and assembled a team to raid the residence.

The hours dragged on. It was near midnight when the phone rang and I heard the familiar voice when I picked up, "Sheila, we got him. Joey is in custody. I do want you to know he is heavily intoxicated, like you said. But we are going to watch him closely all night and then he will be taken to County tomorrow. Hey, we are all here for you."

I cried and barely managed to let the words, "Thank you" escape my lips.

I wrestled with a slight guilt trip of having him arrested on a violation charge. However I could clearly see that the drugs, drinking and depression- maybe caused by the drugs- were taking over Joey's ability to see things rationally. Was it harsh? Yes, it was. What would be harsher though, to make the choice of having your own flesh and blood sent to a jail cell or to have to plan an unnecessary premature funeral service for your child?

He was alive, and that end result was all that mattered.

Chapter Eight

Joey spent the weekend in jail and that following Monday, September 15th; I was on the way--though running late--to get to the court for his arraignment. Before I got there, my cell phone was ringing. It was Jacob, a friend of mine. We had been friends for over twenty-five years. He is a police officer in the city I live in and I knew instinctively that he was calling to tell me something regarding Joey. He asked me if I was on my way to court, and when I told him I was he told me there was no sense in going. He went on to say that Joey had already been brought up in front of the judge and apparently lost his temper and could not keep it together in the courtroom; he threw the table that was in front of him and his attorney. According to Jacob, Joey called the judge stupid, cursed him out, and, hence, was being brought to the county jail on a judiciary contempt of court charge. The judge sentenced him to a month due to his actions. And that kind of charge offers no bail.

I absolutely could not believe what I was hearing. I asked him, "Jacob, what do you mean, he cursed out the judge?"

"Sheila, he cursed him out. He called him all kinds of motherfucker's."

"What!" I asked again in such disbelief. I can't even begin to explain how I felt. I was mortified, to say the least, more than anyone could ever imagine. "Oh, my God! You're kidding me, right?"

"No. Sheila, I'm not kidding. He directly called him a stupid mother fucker."

I then mumbled to him, "What is wrong with this child? What is he thinking? Why does he act this way?" I asked these questions as I drifted into a silent zone for a moment trying so desperately to absorb what Jacob said. His voice quietly, sympathetically, asked me if I was still there on the line, if I was going to be okay.

"Jacob, do you think maybe he is going though with-drawl that he acted that way? Maybe a chemical imbalance is going on? He is so angry. He threatened to kill himself."

Jacob replied, "That's possible. I really don't know what to tell you. But I will be transporting him to county in a little while so I'll talk to him."

I can't believe he did this, I thought to myself. Despite being appalled, all I could say was, "okay."

I had pulled the car over to speak to Jacob and now I just sat there frozen, staring in the rearview mirror, replaying the conversation over again in my head. It was just one thing after another with him and I wondered when it was going to end, if it would ever end. I knew realistically the answer to that question was nightmarishly no time soon.

I contemplated the thought that maybe he acted that way intentionally. Maybe he knew the judge would throw him in jail for that awful behavior. Maybe subconsciously--or consciously---he knew he was getting close to his end, to his breaking point, and maybe it was his way of reaching out for help, a moment of relief from his thoughts, his own demons. I could not help believing that, as extreme as it sounded, for he was, after all, in a very dark place.

Maybe being incarcerated might give him the time he needed to clear his head? He seemed to be already incarcerated within his own mind. Can one ever be free from the demons that notoriously run rampant within one's own thoughts?

While I sat there on the side of the road I decided to call his dad to make him aware of what was going on. I'm not sure why I did but I did. To his own justification, he hadn't been much support to his son, but I felt it a responsibility to let him know what had happened and how Joey had been acting. His son would be in jail for a month and I didn't want him to turn around and say I never informed him.

The last time I had spoken with Travis was when I came home one afternoon from work and he was sitting outside the house in his car waiting for me. I had a sinking feeling when I saw him. I didn't even say hello to him. I instead, immediately asked him what was wrong. He just stared at me for a moment and in that moment it seemed amazing how fast my brain thought and imagined all kinds of scenarios as to what was going on. I didn't know what he was going to tell me. Was Joey in a car accident, in jail, hurt? I guess in retrospect the look was much simpler in its meaning. He just didn't know where to begin telling me what he needed to tell me.

Finally, he said, "We need to talk about your son."

"My son?" I asked with a touch of sarcasm, though at least I knew in my heart that Joey was okay but he obviously did something to piss his father off and it had to be good because he could have just called.

He asked me if I knew his daughter, Joey's half sister, had the baby, and I told him how Joey had called to tell me she was in labor. He went on to tell me that his apartment was broken into that same day, someone had thrown a brick through the window to get in but that nothing was taken except for $3000.00 in cash. I was listening intently to hear it all. He continued on that Joey had left the hospital for a while and so had his daughter's boyfriend. Travis and his now wife believed it was one of them who broke into their home. He said that no one else knew that they were all at the hospital in that time frame.

I could not believe Joey would do this and told him so, how ridiculous was it that his son would do this to him! There was no way I believed this, even knowing how

Joey had stolen many things from my own home, video games, equipment, and cash. Even knowing the level of disrespect he had for this family, which is why he was thrown out in the first place, I just could not believe he would do that.

It wasn't until after Joey caught the burglary charges the following summer on Long Island that I actually entertained the thought, though always in the back of my mind, wondered whether he was capable of doing such a thing to his father. I also was aware that Travis's daughter's boyfriend was known for breaking into people's homes and had an extensive rap sheet for doing so.

It is amazing the depth of denial a mother can have, how far the pain had to take her, before she could open her eyes to the truth of perception, and deception, to accept awareness and be conscious of her child's being who he was and who he was not.

So, as I called his dad and spoke with him about how Joey was being taken down to the county jail for contempt of court due to cursing out the judge and informed him of everything else, the suicide threats, drinking, drugging, etc., he listened and didn't really say much. I think he, himself, was now trying to absorb it all. It's hard to fathom that a child, your child, is acting in a manner that goes beyond the extreme and it's quite disappointing and heart breaking

I finally put the car in gear and pulled out as I pondered the last year, the past six months, and the past few weeks. I thought how quickly I had watched my son nose-dive into the deep end of life where there is no water to break his fall. He was without a doubt going to smash into the concrete bottom and bleed profusely. I could fill the pool with water I suppose so he wouldn't get hurt even though the rest of us would surely suffer. Taking no responsibility for his actions and continuing to be enabled by his own mother, would he have learned anything more than how to manipulate me into picking up the pieces for him over and over again? Would I have learned, if not anything else, other than I am a woman in denial, a mother in denial of having a child with serious problems no matter what the cause?

Not this time. He would fall and he would bleed. He would bleed so much that he would need stitches to help mend his life back together. And as much as a mother's heart aches, I would not be the one who sew-chares him.

Every action has a reaction and every reaction has a consequence. Mine shall be the profound effect it has had on me knowing that the decision I made let him fall into his self-induced wounds. He is still so very young and there is so much hope to be had. My hope for myself is that he knows I love him, how much I love him. But his lifestyle which was controlling ours could not continue. I am helpless in my ability to make everything all better as I could when he was a small child. He needed to admit he needed help. He needed to recognize he had a problem so he could get the therapy he needed if he wanted any chance for any kind of healthy future. He had to make a conscious decision to not want to jump into that deep end.

Chapter Nine

I must say, with little guilt, the past couple of weeks have been peaceful and quiet. I have been sleeping, knowing that Joey cannot get into any trouble, unable to get high or run the streets. So, for at least a little while I can rest.

Though he will only be incarcerated for a month, a month is a long time to be locked behind bars. I am hoping this is all he will need to help him realize he has to make better choices; he has to be responsible for his actions. Jail does not have the comforts of home. He will eat when they tell him to eat. He will shower when they tell him to shower. He will wear the clothes they give him to wear. There are no video games, fluffy pillows, or snacks on demand.

I am hoping during this time he will have an awakening and realize he is worth more and will want more for himself, his future, and his spirit. I am hoping he will want to seek therapy, drug and/or alcohol counseling.

He had mentioned to me a few weeks back that his lawyer on the Island said he will he probably get five years' probation for the burglary charge. I thought that with his having to see a probation officer on a regular basis, it would keep him grounded and forced, for lack of a better word, to remain clean and sober. They would mandate any counseling, if they felt he needed it, which I am sure they would clearly see he needed. I thought we would then be able to put this behind us and move forward. I wondered to myself if it could be that simple.

I had not accepted any of his calls nor had I gone to visit him. He at this point believed it was my fault he was incarcerated. I suppose it was my fault since I threw him out of the house and I refused to allow him to continue to steal from us or allow his violent outbursts to continue for whatever reason he thought it was viable to justify a rage. It would make him feel so powerful to be able to break something just because he could, or so he thought he could; ironically, he couldn't have his way, and he certainly didn't have any power.

I suppose it was my fault he was in jail because he called me saying that things were going to come to a drastic end and I believed in my heart that he was going to end his life, so I did the only thing in my power I could to save him. I certainly had no regrets about it, and over the next month he would have plenty of time to think about whose actions really got him where he was.

I needed to take a harsh stance. As hard as it would be for me to literally turn my back on my child that is what I would have had to do. I needed to make sure the point was vitally clear.

He refused to take any responsibility for his actions. Until he did this family was not going to interact with him. He needed to recognize that besides a substance abuse problem there were anger issues, as well as depression. All these issues were just weighing heavily on him causing all these negative behaviors that were obviously, unhealthy and only leading him to self-medicate.

I hoped that by not going to visit him or sending money or accepting his calls, he would be forced to look within and see the turmoil that he had brought upon himself, as well as the many people who loved him. I hoped he would ask himself why his mother or family wasn't there for him. Or ask himself did he take advantage of everyone one time too many, or tell one lie too much.

He would then make a choice that he may or may not be aware of. That choice might or might not determine our future, but it would with tenacious certainty determine his.

People lie when they cannot face the truth. They fear the truth immensely, especially when poor judgment has been utilized. However, you can never lie to yourself, for your conscious mind which is undeniably powerful, will always know the real truth. This circumstance he was in would hopefully make him able to face that ugly truth within himself and just maybe he would be able to start to heal.

My mother had been visiting him, accepting his calls, and sending him money. Though I understood where she was coming from and felt it mirthless to ask her not to do these things, she felt she needed it. I could almost imagine the arrogance he had, thinking he didn't need me or anything from me. Why should he? He had his grandmother. Then I received this letter:

Dear Mom,   *October '09*

Hey, what's up? I just want you to know I am not blaming you for anything. I know I brought this all on myself. I know you have heard it all before, but all I've done wrong is really eating at me. There's nothing in here for me that I like. I do miss you and everything else about home. I wish I could have done things differently but I just have to man up. I can't whine or cry about nothing. I put myself here. I will do everything in my power to make it up to you guys. I don't want you to think I hate you, because I don't. I love you more than anybody. If it wasn't for you getting me put here-- lol--who knows where I'd be. This is a bad experience but very helpful all the same. I will get it together. You should come see me and send pictures.

Love,

Joey

I was a mom, was I doing the right thing? Every reason I had for it, he had mentioned in his letter.

A seizure was the only word I could think of in relation to how I felt maybe at moments. Sometimes I was calm and life was flowing and I was okay. I had a child with some issues, as did many families, so life kept moving; it didn't stop for me, I had two other sons to take care of, myself, bills, a home, a job. Life wasn't stopping for me, so I would keep it moving as calmly and as best I could.

Then, out of nowhere, my emotional world shook with such force. There was at that moment unbearable sadness. I just started sobbing uncontrollably as I mourned for him. My heart just ached because of the many realms of emotions I went through. One moment I felt sadness, immense sadness, envisioning my son in that dreadful jail cell and sometimes I felt anger for him or towards myself, maybe both. I felt guilty because there must have been something else I could have done so we never would have got to this point.

There are those selfish moments I actually felt relief he was in jail, because we had peace in our lives, or because I knew he was safe but that only brought me back to sadness. So, I got wrapped back up in the calm of my life, which I so much cherish and embrace, until a word or a thought triggered the next seizure because of the anguish caused by convulsions of heartbreaking eruptions that ripped through my body, making my head pound and the tears flow again beyond my control.

On the 36th day of Joey's incarceration I was home on a break getting my things together because I had to go back to work at the salon. The phone rang and it was Joey telling me he was released and my mother had gone to get him. I was relieved he was out but I wasn't ready to see him so I told him I had to get to work, to go on with my mother, and I would call him there in a little while.

A friend of mine had stopped by and we were talking when, a few minutes later, I heard the front door open and a loud voice calling for me, "Mommy, I'm here!" It was Joey, and I was taken aback for a moment. I went towards the front door thinking how I wanted to sit down with him first and see where his head was. We hugged, but it was a strained hug. I asked where my mother was and he said, "Outside in the car."

As I started walking to the front door to see if she was coming in, he realized there was someone else in the house, who happened to be a male friend and Joey started pacing. He blurted out that the court amended the order of protection. Meaning he could come over to the house and be around us as long as he behaved.

He then started to look a bit angry and was saying things I couldn't really make out. I assumed the presence of a male figure was upsetting him. But nothing inappropriate was going on, so I could sense something was going on in his mind but was not quite sure why the sudden change in attitude-not that it was really that surprising. He walked out and slammed the door, then came back in. He started screaming at me that I cared about other people more than him and left the house again. I went outside to see my mother and asked her why she would bring him here. I asked her to get him back in the car and leave. With that, he started cursing at me. He was screaming very loudly in the street, "Fuck you Mom! Fuck you!"

As I walked up the path back to the house, I stopped and turned back to look at him. I told him "Joey, that is the last time you will ever say 'fuck you' to me."

I went in the house and thought it was safe to assume that after all the time he had to think and work on himself and decide what kind of future he would like to have, and the letter he wrote saying he was going to get it together, was, well, apparently, was just the love of a mother hoping he meant those words and was going to return to the person he used to be.

My body leaned against the locked door. I closed my eyes and took a deep breath and listened with my ear against the door to see if I could hear him coming back, but I did not.

I was thinking how fast a month goes by. It was really so peaceful. As the weight of my body pressed harder against the door, I could feel the tears welling up in my eyes as I thought of a quote I once read, *"Perhaps love is the process of my leading you gently back to yourself. Not who I want you to be, but to whom you are."* – Antoine de Saint Exupery

Sheila McGlarry

I knew I was going to need a lot more than just love.

Chapter Ten

After my mother got home with Joey she called me and we spoke briefly. She told me he could stay with her upstate as a determent to his going back to the streets. I felt an enormous amount of relief that he would be there with her, especially since she lived, roughly, an hour away.

I didn't sleep well that night but got up the next morning and went to work as much as I wanted to stay home and take a mental health day. I was quite busy throughout the day at work, which was good since it kept my mind from dwelling on my personal home issues. At one point during the day the phone rang and I heard my boss answer. I heard him saying pleasantly enough, "She's busy right now. I will have her call you back." A moment later I heard my boss say, in a taken back voice, almost questioning the caller, "Fuck me? You just said fuck me? Do me a favor; don't call this phone ever again."

Oh, my God, I thought to myself. It was Joey. No one I worked with was fortunate enough to have anyone be as disrespectful in their life as I have. I was with a client wondering if she had heard the conversation. Of course our self-conscience thinks that everyone hears and knows. For the time being I acted as though I didn't hear anything, quickly starting up a new conversation with her. When I finished with my client, I apologized to Fred for Joey's behavior. He very much understood, and verbally recognized it was not my fault. He knew Joey had some problems. Little did I know how bad the problems were going to get.

I was beyond concerned by now regarding his demeanor. This anger, these outbursts, this crude, harsh, intrusive behavior had been going on for years. It was just becoming so much more regular now; the hatred towards me, his depression and suicide threats, all escalated to a point I was not sure he was capable of coming back from.

Had I been in that much denial? I thought of the past few years. I remember going to a psychic in the Bronx. Joey was about thirteen at the time. She knew nothing about me, not even my name. She told me I had three sons, she even named Joey. I was impressed until she said he was doing drugs. She said he was smoking the funny stuff and I needed to watch his friends. I told her she was wrong, he didn't do drugs; he was into sports – as if kids who play sports don't do drugs. Sitting in her chair, her old eyes held mine as she leaned in towards me, she touched my wrist and the top of my hand and said, "I'm telling you he is doing drugs and he is going to give you a lot of trouble for many years." I will never forget the look in her eyes or the conviction of tone in her voice as she told me that.

A month later a neighbor came to me, he caught Joey smoking pot across the street from his house. It was from that moment forward my son began manifesting into an unknown being.

The next day my mother called me from work to inform me Joey was going to Peekskill. His friends were going up to her house to pick him up. They wanted to go to see a movie and on Sunday they were going to a Giants game and then his friends would bring him back to her house after the weekend. I was in shock. He wasn't at her house

24 hours and already he was heading to Peekskill. I didn't buy it for a minute, I knew by the sinking feeling I had in the pit of my stomach something was wrong. I asked her if she believed him, and she answered that she did. I told her flat out not to expect him to go back to her house after the weekend.

All of a sudden she wanted to call him at her house. We hung up and she called me back only moments later to tell me he was gone. I told her all she could do was wait and see, but I knew my son, I knew his behavior, his deceit, his manipulation, his addiction, his addiction to not just drugs but the streets and his friends. He wasn't going back. I also knew I had to make sure everything was locked and secured here. It might be a very long weekend.

The weekend came and went. I had not heard from Joey and figured he was having a grand time with his friends. He did not even call to wish me a happy birthday, which surprised me. I thought he would at least wish me a happy birthday. I spoke with my mother at some point and she had not heard from him all weekend either. I wondered if she thought he really would have touched base with her.

On Tuesday, October 21st, Joey had a Court appointment on Long Island for the burglary charge. He did not show up and his court appointed lawyer called me to ask me why. [I told her what I thought might have been the truth and that was there was supposed to be a probation report done, which was not, due to him being incarcerated.] I told her I did speak with the probation department on Long Island, who told me court would have to reschedule because of this. I gave her my mother's number and told her she could call her, being Joey was now staying with her. She apparently spoke with my mother that day because my mom called me to say that Joey needed to be in court the next morning or there would be a warrant issued for his arrest. Actually, one already existed but they would recall it if he showed up in court.

My mother must have gotten phone numbers off her Caller ID to reach Joey to tell him about the court date because she showed up at my house very early the next morning saying she was supposed to meet him but he never showed up. She thought maybe she was in the wrong area. She was saying how she worked until 11, and then got up at 4:30 to get ready to meet him and take him. She seemed frantic. Then her cell phone rang. She was asking where he was, then said to stay there, that she was on her way. With that, she was on her way out the door. I hugged her and told her to call me to let me know how things went, because she was not going to bring him back to Peekskill but instead head straight home.

I was off that day so I was around the house doing things. I did a load of laundry, called her cell. I went to the market, I called her cell. I called her cell phone a few more times; there was no answer any time I called.

I was walking into the kitchen, the clock facing me, and the time read 3:43. I was getting ready to start dinner when I looked out the window and saw my mother's truck in the driveway. She was walking up the path so I went to open the door to let her in. I took one look at her and knew she had been crying. I told her to sit down and that I would make her a cup of tea.

I sat down at the table across from her. Her eyes were slightly swollen and red. I was ready to hear he was in jail but that was not the case. She then told me the story of what had transpired. When they got to Long Island she found the courthouse and they went up to the third floor where the courtroom was. They checked in, sat down, and waited for a very long time. At some point Joey's lawyer went to make a phone call and Joey told my mother he would be right back. She waited about twenty minutes and then decided to go look for him. She couldn't find him so returned back to the courtroom in case they called his name. She waited for almost an hour more before she realized or maybe accepted that he wasn't coming back.

In frustration and not understanding why he would do this, she left and made her way back to her truck, where he was in the back seat. She said she asked him what was going on and he told her he was not going to jail. Nothing she said could convince him to go back inside and do the right thing. She told him he was making a big mistake and he told her he wasn't going to jail today or any other day.

She told him if he didn't appear in front of the judge they would issue the warrant for his arrest. He didn't want to hear it.

When they got back to Peekskill, he asked her to drop him off downtown. She said when he got out of the truck he just said he was sorry and walked away.

She stared at her cup of tea. She kept circling the rim of the mug with her finger. She wiped a tear and said, "I'm done. I'm finished now." I remained quiet for the most part. I felt bad that she had worked late, that she got up early, that she had been driving for a total of about five hours, all for him, and he just walked away. I felt bad that I could not fix him. He needed to fix him. I felt bad that it hurt her to have this realization. She sat there and then said, "It's just shocking." She repeated to herself. "It's just shocking."

I asked her in a very soft voice, "Is it, Ma? Are you really shocked?"

"It really is shocking," she said as though she were numb, not really answering me but trying to convince herself.

I wondered if she accepted that he is who she saw today and she could not save him. I wondered if she finally had the slightest inkling of how I felt and what I went through, the deep-rooted hurt, the excruciating disappointments, and the endless, endless painful battles. Her tears told me she did.

Chapter Eleven

That night there was a knock on the door. When I answered it, there was a strange man standing there, "Detective" something. He introduced himself to me as he told me he was looking for Joey to sign papers. I told him Joey wasn't home. I knew he couldn't or at least wouldn't volunteer what the papers were for, so I asked him if they were my order of protection papers, and he said, "Yeah. Do you know where I can find him?" I knew he was lying, because Joey had signed them when he was in the Peekskill Court and I already had received them, so I knew the papers he was talking about were arrest warrant papers from Long Island for his not showing up in court. I told him I had no clue where he was; he could be with any one of his friends.

He said, "If you hear from him, can you have him go to the police department?"

"Sure," I said, even though I hadn't spoken to Joey since the day he cursed me out.

So now I knew the arrest warrant was officially issued and the police up here were aware of it. There was nothing anybody could do to help him, not my mother, not his attorney. It was only a matter of time before he was picked up and would have to face the consequences of his actions. He just kept digging a deeper and deeper hole for himself. I wondered why some people were so self-destructive. Why did people choose to make their lives harder than they had to be?

October 30th, my mother called me to say Joey had called her and he had been arrested in Peekskill. He was picked up on a bench warrant. That was fast, I thought to myself. She wanted to know what would happen, so I told her I would call the police station and inquire.

Instead, I went down there. My friend Jacob came out to talk to me as if he was waiting, knowing I would show up. Joey had been arrested on the grounds of the bench warrant but also for resisting arrest and obstruction of governmental property. He told me that he ran from the police and into a building, where he ran up to the third floor and was unable to escape, that's where he put up the resistance and was finally apprehended.

I really wasn't shocked. He had a look on his face and in his eyes like he had more to say. The words that fell from my friends' lips next were what I found incredibly humiliating. He was humiliated for me. Grotesque as it was, I stood there appalled intently listening as I could see the concern and hurt in his eyes as he struggled passing the pain onto me, so not wanting to tell me the behavior of my child after he was brought to the station.

Jacob thought Joey appeared to be on something, maybe Dust. He had to justify Joey's nasty accusations. He said Joey started off by accusing one of the officers of calling him derogatory and racial names. He was accusing one of the officers of wanting to have sex with his mother. He kept screaming that the officer just wanted to fuck me and that the officer wanted me to suck his dick. I felt sick. I could feel the stares of the officers as they passed through, looking at me like they felt so sorry for me. Their minds were aching to know, though, if there was any truth to the words Joey was spitting out of his filthy mouth.

I stood there in a very surreal moment as though I wasn't really there. Kind of like floating, watching someone else's life, certainly not mine. Listening but not quite hearing the depth of the words because it was like a bad dream and hurt so deeply to know my own son could speak of me in such a manner that was so degrading. The words only confirmed in my mind the hatred he had for me. How could anyone say such things about their own mother without possessing hate?

Jacob tried to change the subject letting me know that Joey would be brought to court November, 3d, for the new charges. After facing the consequences of those charges he will then be brought to Long Island to deal with the burglary charges there.

He was speaking, but I didn't really comprehend anything after the ugly words he had told me.

My mind was still repeating that part of the conversation. I interrupted him and had to end the conversation because I needed to get out of there. I could feel nothing but disgust. I felt so sick.

My mother called me over the weekend to let me know Joey had called her saying the arresting officer had called him a stupid motherfucker, a mixed breed, and other names. She was very upset, talking about calling the NAACP and filing complaints against the police department. I just couldn't handle it right then. I told her I needed time to think because I wasn't going to justify anyone's actions but I knew my son and he was certainly no angel. At that moment in time I could just not go to bat for him.

I told my mother what he said at the police station about me and another officer. She seemed shocked but I could sense a bit of animosity from her. This animosity coming from a woman who was saying she was done with him not more than two weeks ago! We hung up the phone both feeling the tension.

When November 3d came, I could not bring myself to go to court for his hearing. My mother went, though, and she sat and waited for his name to be called. It never was. Eventually she asked the court officer what was going on with his case. He told her Joey was not being brought up to court to see the judge because he was freaking out and had to be double-cuffed. Apparently he was acting in a violent manner, threatening to kick asses, and nearly breaking the door of the holding cell, so because of his obtrusive behavior his court date would be rescheduled until the 10th of the month, when, maybe, he would be able to control his emotions.

My mother came after court to tell me all this. The only word that came to my mind as my mother related the story was insanity. This whole entire saga was just insane. There was no other word, no explanation, just insanity in its purest form, and I was at a point where I needed to disconnect from it. If my mother wanted to continue to be a part of Joey's life, then that was her decision. I was not up for any more emotional torture, repulsive insults, embarrassments, let downs, or heart aches.

My mother, who was contemplating calling the NAACP went on to mention she had grabbed her mail on the way down to me and looked at it briefly. As she was driving, she had an urge to pull over to check out one of the envelopes more closely. She opened it up and realized it was a statement from a credit card she never used. She kept this particular card for emergencies only. There were hundreds and hundreds of dollars of charges. I already knew without being told who the obvious responsible party was. She told me what the charges were for and the dates. I instantly thought how he must have taken it when he was up at her house for the one day before his friends came and got him. There were numerous charges to restaurants, gas stations, clothing stores, the movies, etc.

She, once again, could not believe it. I reminded her of how much he had stolen from me, cash, game systems and games; anything that could be sold on the street he sold I told her, "I'm his mother and he stole from me. Did you think you would be different?" I wondered when this insanity was going to stop.

I told her at that moment I would not support any complaint she made to the police department, the NAACP or anyone else. Whether that police officer did or did not say those things to Joey, which certainly was not acceptable, I do know all the things Joey has said and done to me and to others and I just cannot stand up for him at this point.

Chapter Twelve

I went to a little café in the middle of town across the street from the theater. It was a very peaceful place for me. I could relax and fall into the throes of a book or write in a journal. The outside world became non-existent to me. People came and went but I heard no one. I didn't hear my heart crackling with broken emotions of my family, my eldest son. I didn't even hear my own thoughts as they banged across the frontal lobe of my brain.

I ordered one of their high-in-calories caramel-flavored coffees with whipped cream on top and found a settee to get comfortable on.

I had found a copy of James Frey's *A Million Little Pieces* in a local used book store. I had wanted to read it since all the attention it received was both fascinating because of the story behind the man and the controversial, man behind the story. I didn't care about how harsh the press had been on him for maybe fictionalizing some of his story; it was still his story. It was his story of addiction and the battles he went through, though I was searching for maybe more of the battles his parents and family went through and maybe an understanding of why addiction held him and why he couldn't let go.

After reading quite a few pages, I had put the book down to take a sip of my coffee, which was not so hot now but still tasty. My mind wandered as I stared outside the window into life outside. How many people embark on the battle of their life because of addiction? I could already feel a powerful connection to this story. I couldn't put the book down.

I wanted to know more about him, more so his parents. I knew I could feel their pain and share the powerless ability to not be able to help their own child. In spite of all the hardships I wondered will they still be there, are they still there, hoping, loving, forgiving, or enabling maybe?

I was thinking my son's addiction is nothing like this man's. Then I felt scared because this guy's bottom was horrendous, almost seemingly impossible for any human being to go through. Is this how far down into the depths of poison that some have to endure? I wondered if for some it will even be maybe a never ending-cycle of being reborn into the addiction over and over and over again, being cradled and protected by the arms of cocaine and Hennessy so that you will never have to face the reality of being sober and dealing with all the pain that has been caused.

I wondered aimlessly at the different events and choices I had made in my life. I searched relentlessly to find blame within myself. So many people say you can't blame yourself for your child's actions. They say your child will make his or her own choices. How many times have I heard it is not my fault? But aren't we, as parents somewhat responsible for the path they choose? I think we are...somewhat.

To enable someone, we allow them to do something. We give them power. We sit and say nothing, or maybe we do, but nothing of significance anyway. We do nothing that will make them stop in their tracks and question the outcome of their actions and nothing that will make them take an inner look at themselves. We can do nothing that overpowers the hold that addiction has on them. There are no consequences for them, only for us, the enabler. We endure the never-ending cycle. They, the addicts continue to do whatever it is that they have been allowed to do and proceed to hurt, drink, drug, abuse, destroy, lie, steal, ravage, and when confronted, exhibit excruciating sorrowfulness. With our obscured vision, we recoil, forgive, restore, rescue, love endlessly, we hope endlessly, and the cycle so continues.

My child, I do take responsibility for your choices. My child, I failed you. I enabled you to continue on a path of internal destruction. I thought I did everything I could to save you, and perhaps I did, but I did it too late; I tried too late. I should have educated you to your shortcomings. I should have made you accept responsibilities for your actions sooner in life, when you were younger, not at nineteen, when you felt you didn't have to answer to me. It was too late then. It was too late at eighteen. It was too late at seventeen. I'm trying to search and see when it was too late to save you. Denial embraced me and held me so tight that when you were fourteen and I was putting your laundry away and found an empty bottle of Hennessy in your drawer I blew it off that it was normal teenage curiosity to sneak liquor and drink. Why didn't I put my foot in your ass then? That's what I should have done. Instead, I just threw the bottle out.

Or the time I came home early to find you barricaded in your room with your friends smoking weed. I was so angry, the audacity you had smoking in our home. I should have put my foot in your ass that day. I yelled, you blew me off and left. I shouldn't have let you leave.

I failed you. I failed you….my sweet little boy who used to laugh, who loved to play football, who was a wonderful artist, and now, because I have unconsciously enabled you to drink and get high, by my being in a world of denial, you have a life of struggles within yourself ahead of you. My son, I failed. How excruciating it is to have that realization and to accept it.

Chapter Thirteen

Would a mother ever wish for her child to be in jail? Sadly, I do. I don't want him having a criminal record, but he needs a place that is safe, a place where his mind can be clear and his body free of drugs. Not to say I think jail is a safe environment or the best of places to clear one's mind, but it is, sadly, his only option at the moment. Prison is the end result of bad choices made. He's not on the streets, where he would only continue on his path of self-destruction.

My heart has broken. I have cried tears of a lifetime for this child. He is going to have to face his demons and, hopefully, conquer them, hopefully want to conquer them. Only he can do that by looking inside himself and wanting to end this drug-induced nightmare that he has manifested into his reality. Whatever time he has to serve, he just has to serve, and maybe he will make positive strides within himself with that time.

November 10th, Joey was brought back to court to face the charges of resisting arrest and destruction of governmental property. I was sitting in the front row. As they called his name my eyes fixated on the side door, where they brought in the prisoners. He entered the room and would not look at me. It was quite fast. The judge, the court-appointed attorney, Ms. Hudson, who was very intelligent and really cared about Joey getting the best defense he was entitled to, and the DA, agreed to delay sentencing until December eight. As he exited the side door he never looked back.

It was very sad for all of us to have Joey miss Thanksgiving dinner. That one special day that people gave thanks for the loved ones in their life, their family and friends, health, the ability to love, and the ability to forgive, the warm glorious meal they got to sit down to together and enjoy, but for us Joey would not be a part of it.

December's court day approached, and again, I was in the front row. When Joey entered the courtroom this time he did not ignore me, he glanced at me and smirked. His attorney and the DA approached the bench, they spoke to the judge, would look at each other and speak, nod heads, and then return to their seats. The judge spoke and said that they would all return to court regarding this matter on January 29th. Joey's face went red. He rolled his eyes, pierced his lips together, and shook his head. He believed he would have been released before Christmas, but even if he was released, he forgot he would go directly to Long Island. As the court officer led Joey out of the court room he yelled out loud and sarcastically, "Happy Holidays!" The judge looked in Joey's direction and just shook his head. I knew this was the one young man the judge would always remember.

Ms. Hudson took me aside and explained to me that Joey was given a "Parker Warning" when arraigned originally on Long Island, which meant that he could not get arrested more than one time while the case was pending. If he did, the offer of probation would be off the table. She wanted to call the attorney who was handling the case for him on Long Island to see now what would happen being that he had this trouble going on. She said she would see what she could do so that he did not have to do years in prison because of these charges.

Now Christmas was approaching and there would be a place-setting missing at the dinner table as with Thanksgiving. How would I keep this family together through all of this? How would I keep my other two children's spirits up throughout all this, knowing their brother was so heavy on their minds? How would I keep it together? In spite of Joey's ill behavior, he was still my son and their brother and it would be a Christmas without him. In spite of me and him not having a very good or even healthy relationship at this moment in time, he was my son and he should have been here with us, not waking up in a jail cell on Christmas morning.

When he was a child, he would always be the first one up and he would come running into my room to tell me Santa had come. Even as he grew older into his teen years he would come in my room to wake me, to ask me if he could wake up his brothers. Even as a big child that excitement still thrived in him. There would be no one this year to sneak down the stairs and shake the presents under the tree. There would be no presents for him under the tree this year. How would I get through this?

Regardless of the sadness, heartache and disappointments, the anger, resentments, fury, even in knowing that his behavior was due to his addiction, I decided that I was still not going to visit him in jail, not even for Christmas.

Someone actually said to my face that I have given up on him. I certainly was happy that this person has never had to experience this path in life. However I had not given up; I had to take a stance. I had to inflict tough love. I needed to make the message clear to him. He had to realize that if this is the life he wanted, stealing, drugging, boozing, manipulating, lying, and thieving, this tumultuous, self-destructive behavior then he would live this life of his by himself. He would not have his mother or brothers, and as heavy-hearted as it would be, it would just be.

I had not given up but I can say I had become disconnected. I don't think a mother can ever give up, but a woman can disconnect.

The New Year had come in. We normally had a party with our family and friends, good food and Champagne, and sweet treats, like chocolate pastry puffs, chocolate strawberries, and a chocolate fountain full of things to dip in it.

Instead, this year was a relatively quiet one by choice, simple and peaceful. I needed it to be on the quiet side. I couldn't celebrate happiness and joyous times knowing I was hurting and suffering inside for what felt like the loss of a son.

Instead, I brought the New Year in with hopes and dreams for a better year for all. I prayed for my sons. I prayed for my son. I prayed for me. I prayed to be a better mother, a wiser woman. I prayed to be stronger, devoted and conscious. I believe that our one life, our one precious life, is a gift but also a choice, a conscious choice of how we want our life to be. I do believe there are two kinds of people in this world, the unconscious and the conscious, or the unaware and the aware.

I prayed--oh, how I prayed--for my son to become conscious of his being, his life, his spirit. That he should wake up and realize he only had this one life. I wanted him to want more for himself and not necessarily for his future but for now, his present. I needed him to want more for himself now, to learn from his mistakes now, so he could maybe get some joy and happiness from his one precious life.

Chapter Fourteen

One night I was in bed and it was around 10:30 when the phone rang. I wasn't going to get it but something nudged at me to. When I answered, it was Joey calling. He asked about his brothers and even my mother, though she had gone to visit him a few times. It was January 10th and this was only the second time we had spoken in many, many weeks, as our relationship was obviously, strained, which you could hear in the silence.

He asked me if I was going to go visit him, and I told him no. He wasn't surprised and he moved on to talk about something else. We spoke about the weather and his pending case on Long Island. In the middle of a sentence he threw out that he keeps hanging up on his attorney there, as if he had to confess to me.

I asked him why and his response was simply, "She pisses me off!" He clearly didn't want to hear me lecture him and there was a moment of silence. In that moment I was thinking how he had not learned anything yet. He hadn't seemed to have taken one step forward or made any growth to internally progress in a positive manner in how he handled situations or people, especially the people who wanted to help him.

He finally asked me why I was quiet, and I immediately instinctively thought that we were about to have an argument because he could not take constructive criticism or advice; he could not be told that he shouldn't be doing something or that he should do something, or especially be told that he was being disrespectful. I thought carefully how to choose my words but then thought sometimes it just didn't matter. And this was one of those times. We were going to disagree and he would either hang up on me or me on him, and no matter who hangs up on who he would call me repeatedly until I couldn't take it anymore and I would have to turn the phone off.

      I prepared myself for the psycho cycle, the unhealthy mother/adult-child relationship that was once again about to wreak havoc on me, and his mere lack of self-constraint would pluck at every nerve I had.

      I decided to make him think as to why he did the things he did. I wanted to make him say it as opposed to my saying it. Maybe he wouldn't or couldn't get angry with me this way. So, I asked him in the calmest voice I could muster, what exactly pissed him off that it caused him to hang the phone up on his attorney. His response was simple, "I get angry." I explained to him that it was not her fault that he was in the position he was, she was there to counsel him, and he needed to learn to have a civil conversation with her if he wanted to be able to understand what was going to happen regarding his very near and approaching future in the Long Island Correctional Facility.

She was telling him he was facing one and a half to four years in prison; there was an offer of probation but because he was rearrested that was no longer a valid option for him. He blamed everyone but himself for all the bad things that had happened to him over the last few years. There was no sense of self-responsibility and no bothersome consciousness for the lack of one.

This was the first time we had spoke in quite a while. I did want to be there for him, but he made it so difficult. Again, I chose my words selectively and gently told him that maybe he needed to be more polite with her on the phone and show her a little more respect.

It was amazing how I could feel his attitude start to transition over the phone, from that simple statement I made to him. I could sense he was twittering on edge, trying so hard to refrain from being defiant to my advice. His tone was getting a little icier. I could almost envision his changing demeanor, as he had stood before me so many times and would get that look in his eyes, those dark brown eyes turning almost black with wrath, imploding as his veins grew thicker from the blood that was curdling inside of him, then exploding with raging fists into walls and a mouthful of curses and disgust, ranting, raving, ejecting nothing but vile upon me, his mother.

I tried to change the subject so to avoid what was approaching. I brought up that he was going to be sentenced in Peekskill on the 29th of January and that I would be there. He would probably be sentenced to time served and released. I told him his brother did have a doctor's appointment but that I would reschedule it.

He said, "You don't need to come to court, Ma." I asked him what was wrong and his answer was in a very numbing, unemotional tone, "Fuck you, Mom."

Not surprised, I knew it was coming the moment I told him to be nicer to his attorney. But then again he could have said it was raining and I could have told him not to forget his umbrella and the end result would have been the same.

"You know what Joey, don't call me anymore." I hung up the phone. Before I went to bed, I unplugged the phone wire so I didn't have to listen to him calling six times to yell and curse into the machine. I knew I would not sleep the rest of the night; I would twist and turn and wonder why he acted in such a manner. I asked myself if I meant what I said to him. I wondered maybe how many more weeks would go by before he would call and I would pick up the phone. This cycle never seemed to end. I wondered if this was how our relationship was going to be for the next two years, five years, or twenty years. I wondered if this was the drugs making him act this way or was it the withdrawal. Would he mature and start to make more reasonable and responsible decisions? Or would he always be irrational and illogical, bordering on the brink of insanity when it came to reacting to dilemmas, trials and tribulations?

I was so scared for him but I was so angry at him. If he felt he could disrespect me, his mother, he would feel he could disrespect anyone. He was too comfortable in believing that he could curse at me. He cannot say 'fuck you" to me; he cannot say it anymore.

I lay in bed convincing myself that each time I said, "I'm done," I did mean it, but he was my son and I, like most mothers, in spite of whatever issues, faults, misconduct and indiscretions my children have, know they are still my children. We are codependents to their needs, to our need of the unconditional love we give to them, but we are not helping them by condoning their behavior or habitually forgiving them without necessarily, verbally doing so. They just know, and, unfortunately, so do we, and the cycle so continues.

Chapter Fifteen

I had a pain that would not cease. I ached for my first child to want to love life in a normal, healthy, functioning way. I did not want my son to be a thief, or a burglar, or a drug dealer. I wanted him to want to be the best he could be no matter what profession he chose. I didn't want him breaking into people's homes and stealing money. I didn't want him going to prison. I wanted my baby boy home in his bed, safe, and his stomach full, not living in the streets because he gave me no choice but to throw him out to them because he just kept taking and taking, and abusing and abusing, and taking and abusing.

I had a pain that would not cease. My heart ached for my son who thought he knew everything and yet he knew nothing. He didn't realize it even though I had told him so many times the path he was choosing was going to lead him right to where he was at right now.

Every time I watched Oprah I felt she was talking to me. Her spirit was enlightening. I then discovered a very compelling author, Robin Sharma, who had become my life coach and healer through his books. I had joined a support group for parents with troubled children. I had learned to become conscious of my situations, of my world, and the people in it. I had learned to recognize what I needed to change. I could not change someone else but I could change me, and how I reacted to people.

Knowing Joey's court date was approaching, I did everything that week without concentration. I had kind of floated through, functioning barely, coherent barely, sleeping barely, thinking of nothing except Joey's appearance in front of the judge on the next day, January 28th. I thought of our conversation and how he spoke to and cursed at me. I questioned myself as to why I should even go to court and be there for him. But he was my child; I had to be there for him. I had to continue to fight for him even when he wouldn't fight for himself.

I knew for sure that when the judge sentenced him to time served and then made him aware that he would be remanded until the Long Island police picked him up that he would surely freak out. Maybe he would see me in court and start screaming and cursing, blaming me for all of this, though in reality he was in jail right now for cursing out a judge. I suppose it was my fault. I was so frustrated and so hurt. But this was how it was going to play out.

A little after three in the afternoon on January 30th, I was getting the boys a snack before dinner when the phone rang. It was Joey calling from the Long Island Police Department waiting to be brought over to the Riverhead Correctional Facility. He spoke with his brothers for a minute or so, then I spoke with him and told him to be strong and to pray for strength and guidance. We hung up and I broke down crying hysterically. This was the beginning of a lot more pain. This is where all the misdemeanor charges were completed and he now faced the music with a felony charge and the possibility of going upstate to prison.

I sat at the kitchen table with my head face down in my arm and just cried and cried. My littlest guy tried to console me, but I was inconsolable. I reached up to hug him and it just made me cry more. I thought of when Joey was small like this one. He was so sweet and happy all the time. He never stole anything from stores or told lies; he was a good boy, and never in a million years would I have thought my son, my child, my baby boy, would grow up to be accused of breaking into someone's home and stealing money from them.

I thought about how in the Westchester County Jail he sadly, but thankfully, knew a few people in there. In the Riverhead Jail he knew no one. There was not one soul to watch his back. And at that thought I cried even harder and held my youngest son even tighter. I could feel my other son's hand rubbing my back and I reached one arm around him and I just cried and hugged both my children.

The pain would just not cease. As I hugged my sons, the pain hugged me back. It gripped me and intertwined every part of my body like an ivy vine that grew and spread its roots, manifesting deep within, and I could not escape it. The pain was creeping through me, searching for my heart, wanting, I know, to crush it, wanting to destroy me.

At that moment I pulled back and looked at my two children standing over me. I wiped my tears and remembered that I could not change other people but I could change me; I had two other sons that I had to be able to focus on out here in the real world. They depended on me and I had to be able to keep it together. I had to stop barely doing anything and give my all to everything, because that is who I am and that is what they know, and need.

Chapter Sixteen

An analogy of my emotions in regards to my son would be like a never-ending roller coaster ride that goes through loops and tunnels, that being Joey's attitude, then flows straight, and just when I thought he was on the right path flipped me upside down; his anger and lack of self-control kicked in and the ride spun me backwards. It moved straight again, a brief moment of calm seemingly so that it might just come to an end. Then all of a sudden it jerked and made a sharp turn. Joey has had a meltdown. Then there is calm when the ride started to slow down, and as though God had finally responded to my prayers it had finally stopped and there was peace but yet with that peace there was sadness because Joey was in jail.

As the weeks went by while Joey was incarcerated, I waited to hear how much time he would serve. I selfishly admitted that I was a bit happy because there was peace in the house, I was able to function, there was no drama, and I could sleep at night. Selfishly, yes, I was finding a little piece of happiness, and I was peaceful and functioning.

It was sad and embarrassing and so humiliating to say my child broke into some person's home. It hurt to admit out loud that he had a drug problem. Or worse, that he had had this problem for a while and I never saw it. Or worse, I did see it and denied it and now he was engulfed in addiction and legal problems and I was engulfed in heartache. It was sad that the probability of his spending a few years in prison was a reality that this whole family would have to deal with and it was humiliating that I would at times have to explain where he was to people.

I didn't want my neighbors, friends, family, or anyone knowing. If someone asked me where he was, I would respond with an answer that he was finding himself. Most people smiled and made a face as if they were saying, "I have one of those at home," as if they could relate. Little did they know, they certainly could not relate.

The weeks continued to go by and I had really made a conscious effort to be there for him. When he called I tried to give him words of hope and encouragement regarding his future after he got released. If he said something insulting to me, I tended to let it go only because I was trying to be sensitive to his situation, so I would bite my tongue and the weeks continued to go by until his sentencing.

It was Tuesday, March 2nd, 2009. This was the day Joey would find out his fate. I waited anxiously for the phone to ring for him to tell me what the verdict was. It wasn't too far into the afternoon when he finally called. His voice sounded excited and I could sense the obvious, that his sentencing wasn't too bad. I actually thought for a moment he was going to tell me that he was being released though I couldn't see how, logically that could be possible.

"Ma, I'll be home June 26th! They gave me six months with time served since I've been here and I'll have five years' probation." I couldn't believe how lucky he was. I told him how happy and relieved I was for him. I spoke to him about lessons learned and his future. I explained to him that I wanted him to go live upstate with my mother, and he willingly agreed. We both knew if he came back here the streets would surely get him again.

While we were on the phone he was arguing with another inmate. I asked him what that was about and he said the guy was nobody and not to worry about it. I told him to stay to himself and avoid any confrontations.

I continued talking to him about getting his license and other positive things that would help him to get back on the right track. He abruptly told me he would call me back and ended the call.

Two minutes later he called back. I asked him what happened and he told me that some guy in the same dorm area as he was in, was ignorant; the guy could dish out jokes and insults but couldn't take it when given back to him. I thought it was strange he referred to jail as a dorm, but didn't comment on it. Instead I told him to stay away from that guy and not to be joking with people since they are probably more sensitive than normal and might react physically.

During our conversation he broke away from me saying, in a sarcastic tone to someone, "What? What?" A pause then, "So what you wanna do?"

"Please, Joey, stop. Don't pay him any attention. He wants a reaction from you and you are giving it to him."

He was ignoring me but then started yelling into the phone, "Ma! Ma!" He was calling me like he needed me. He was calling me like he hadn't in so many years. I heard two voices, one being his. They were muffled as if Joey had his hand over the mouth-piece on the phone. I was now yelling into the phone, "Joey? Joey?" I heard cursing and yelling and threats being made in the background. I cried, "Joey please, please just ignore him!" Then Joey made a sound I never heard before, a sharp grunt type of sound. Something took him by surprise as if his breath had been taken away from him in an instant, a gasp.

"Joey, please answer me! Joey?" Then I heard a scratchy sound. The mouth-piece was brushing up against something. And then all I heard was the dial tone.

"Joey!" I sat down on the coffee table in the living room staring at the phone, listening to the dial tone until it went silent.

The reality that I had heard my own child possibly hurt and fearful put me in shock. My mind kept replaying the words and the sounds. Maybe I was wrong, I thought, as the tears rolled down my face.

I couldn't do anything; I couldn't talk, I couldn't think, I couldn't focus. I paced around the house not aware of anything but the noises I had heard on the phone. That gasp, what caused it, I wondered. The grunt and then the gasp, two haunting sounds.

He wasn't calling back and I sat on the couch for hours frozen and praying that everything was okay. The boys had come from school and went to their dad's house and I still just lay on the couch praying and wondering.

Finally the phone rang and it was Joey, "Hey, Mom. I'm okay. Are you all right?"

He explained to me that he was sorry, that I had no idea what was going on and that it took him a while to get back to me. He said he couldn't call me back right away because he had to go to the infirmary. The guy that he was having a problem with had stabbed him in the abdomen while we were on the phone.

I felt drained. I was crying on the phone and he was saying he was fine and will be okay. He said he was lucky that where he was stabbed didn't penetrate deep enough to hit anything, but that he would have a small scar. The inmate who had stabbed him was younger than him and getting ready to go upstate to prison for eight years for stabbing someone else. Joey kept assuring me that he was going to be a little sore but he would be all right.

One of my worst fears had come to fruition. The gasp was one of the most powerful sounds I have ever heard in my life. The silence that followed when the phone went dead silenced my being as a mother.

Chapter Seventeen

The weeks that passed since Joey had been incarcerated and stabbed, I was trying to work on our relationship via letters and phone calls. I knew it had been a life-altering lesson for him and through his letters I saw he felt that way, but through his words in our conversations I thought they begged to differ.

When he called on April 14th he sounded pretty good. He'd been counting the days until he would be released and on this day there would only be forty more days to go. We were discussing that I would send him money to get home on the Metro-North from Grand Central Station in Manhattan. He made a comment that, "They'd better pay my way home. I didn't ask to come out to this jail."

I was appalled at his audacity. "What? They didn't ask for you to commit a crime in their town," I said. He laughed. Trying to change the subject, he asked me to call a friend of his on three-way.

I never listened in on a conversation before but something was tugging at me to listen to this one and I couldn't believe what I was hearing. His friend Lou was filling him in on which friend was doing time, who got stabbed, who got busted in a sale, and who got caught with a gun. When they hung up, I said, "Joey," in a clear tone that let him know, I was not happy.

"I know, Ma," was all he could reply.

I hung up the phone and said, "God help this child."

I received a letter from him on April 24th here is an excerpt of it: *"Being locked up is not for me, not at all. So many people I know are locked up, have been locked up, or are most likely going to have that locked-down experience one day. Sad to say, I have a few cousins that are locked up right now and one of my best friends is in for armed robbery. I went to visit him one time and then I got wrapped up in my own world. I have a cousin in jail for twenty-five years and another one for twenty. The neighborhoods in New York are fucked up. Maybe it's just New York in general."*

I understood how he perceived the way he grew up and what was around him, but there was also good there and a lot of it. There were so many neighborhoods all over the country that were crack-infested, crime-riddled and full of gang-bangers but these neighborhoods were not in existence by themselves, they fall in the laps of nice neighborhoods and we had to be responsible for our own choices.

Reading this letter and others, did not give me the impression that he had taken responsibility for his mistakes, and when there was no remorse of errs, how would someone move forward in a positive light? I believed the five years' probation the Courts ordered him to do upon his release was just a long noose for him to hang himself with.

My mother always told me, "Show me who your friends are and I will show you who you are." When you have friends who commit crimes, you are most likely to do so. He had some great friends and I hoped that when he got out that s would be who he would interact with.

I went through a few weeks of internal turmoil of an onerous state trying to prepare myself for his impending release, well aware that the past couple of months were very nice. I was slowly building our relationship back up to something decent, amazed that something almost irreparable, because it had been destroyed by words and actions, could return to this level. It was comforting to be able to converse with my son and not be afraid that being truthful with him would cause animosity. It was so comforting that it almost had a falsehood about it.

As May strolled in, I was feeling anxious and edgy. We were having more and more conversations before the time he was in incarcerated came to an end. I appreciated the time we had to rebuild but I was nervous that he would fall apart soon after being released. I felt guilty for feeling that way, but he was my son, and every mother knows her child more than they know themselves.

Memorial Day Weekend was approaching and I decided to get out of town with the boys. Joey would be home the following Tuesday and I thought the boys and I needed some "us" time and time for me to prepare them and settle any issues they might have. I took them to Washington, D.C., where it would be both educational and fun. My girlfriend and her kids wanted to go as well, so we decided to go together. I wanted my sons to know that I was here for them also and no matter what happened in the future they could always trust and count on me. That I needed them to feel connected to me and me to them and knew the long weekend getaway would be perfect.

My youngest was excited that his oldest brother would soon be home so we could be a family again. Anthony, son No 2 was not so excited. He had been quiet and internalizing what might be. I felt his pain and his anxiety. He was well aware of Joey's rage, as he had been the target of it for a very long time.

The minute I got into the car and started the five-hour drive to Washington I felt a sense of relief. The boys were excited and didn't even mind getting up at five in the morning. I knew this trip would be especially good for Anthony.

We stayed in a studio apartment right in the heart of the Capital. We visited all the museums. We saw the Washington Monument, the Washington Mall, and the Lincoln Monument. We watched Rolling Thunder, which was thousands of motorcycles riding down Independence Avenue paying tribute to all the men and woman who had and who were currently serving this country. There was a point where the boys started yelling out "thank you" to them as they passed by. My eyes filled with tears because I was so proud that they were aware and acknowledged these people's sacrifices.

Being with the boys and experiencing the history of that city was just amazing. They forgot all about Joey coming home. Anthony had no stress and all I saw when I looked at him was joy. His eyes just beamed with happiness.

On Memorial Day we took the subway over to the White House, and as soon as the kids saw it they ran over to the gates. We took tons of pictures and walked around. I couldn't bring myself to bring up any conversations about Joey coming home. There was just no perfect moment.

I was standing on the corner waiting for my girl-friend and all the kids to get a drink from a vendor when all of a sudden police cars swooped in and blocked off the road. A police motorcycle sped in and parked ten feet from me.

I felt fear and panic rush through me, not knowing what was going on. The officer stayed on the bike and was looking at me. I looked back to my girlfriend and the kids to see what they were doing and to call them closer to me. I looked back at the police officer on the bike, but my eyes searched past him. Looking past him, in the background I saw huge iron gates opening slowly and then it hit me where we were. The panic I felt quickly surged into excitement and I started screaming to everyone that I thought the President was coming out! We stood there focusing cameras as each vehicle in the Presidential motorcade came out. In amazement, in utter awe, President Obama looked at us and waved to us as he drove out. We all started yelling with even more excitement.

As the weekend came to an end and we hit the road to go home, none of us thought of the next day that was ahead of us. We revisited every moment of our trip on the way home and counted how many different license plates we saw from other states. The boys and I had an unbelievable weekend that created wonderful memories for us.

I hoped that the weekend would stay with the boys for their lifetime. I hoped if things got difficult, those memories would bring a bit of joy to them. I hoped they would keep within them the happiness we felt as a family and more so the love and peace we felt together at that moment.

I hoped and prayed that the next day forward and thereafter Joey would be able to change his life, be a part of this family, and be a positive role-model for his younger brothers, that happiness and peace would therefore, remain.

Chapter Eighteen

Coming back into New York was damp and cold. It had been so hot in Washington, the sun just beamed on us the whole time we were there. By the time the boys and I got home we were exhausted, leaving our bags in the foyer and simultaneously heading up the stairs to our individual bedrooms. Not one of us brushed our teeth, washed our face, or got clothes out for the next day.

The minute my head rested on the pillow I fell into an unconscious state. When the alarm clock went off I awoke and thought for a few minutes that I would just lie in bed thinking of the wonderful weekend I had with the boys.

Then, as if with a jolt to the right hemisphere of my brain, I suddenly remembered that it was May 26, 2009 and today Joey would be released from prison. This was a clean slate for him; this was how I told myself to look at it. Even with his track record over the past few years, I shouldn't hasten the thought, which would only be fair. As his mother, if I didn't take that attitude with him, who would? If I didn't have faith in him, would he have faith in himself?

Everyone deserves a chance to make his or her life right. I had given a good degree of thought to this silently over this past weekend. Joey was supposed to go live with my mother, but I would have really loved to let him stay here with us and see if we could move forward and continue to develop our relationship and live as a family unit. He would be able to develop a wonderful relationship with his younger brothers and slowly maybe mold into a positive role-model for them. I wanted to guide my son into the next chapter of his life.

I got up out of bed and got the boys up because they did have school. They were both exhausted but got up without a fight because they were both very excited to get to school and share their experiences with their friends. I think they were really eager to tell their friends about seeing President Obama waving to us.

I myself debated about taking the day off since, being away all weekend, I hadn't gone food shopping and was sure Joey would want some good home-cooking. I knew there was a whole process Joey had to go through before actually being released, and then he would have to make his way to Penn Station, then Grand Central, and another hour after that, so I dropped the boys off at school and reluctantly decided to go to work.

The morning seemed endless before Joey called to say what time he would be home. When he finally arrived in Peekskill and called, I answered the phone; his voice was jumping with excitement, "Mommy! Mommy!" He talked so fast I couldn't manage to respond. "I love you, Mommy!" I heard a click and then the dial tone. I thought to myself it was a very good thing I understood him.

Later in the day, on my way to the train station to pick him up, I realized all the different feelings I felt. I almost felt intoxicated with all the different emotions running through me. I was excited for him that he was being released. I couldn't even imagine what it was like for him and what it felt like for him right now. I was joyful that he was at the footpath of a new beginning. I was anxious, so anxious. I was concerned and I was hopeful. Of all the emotions I was feeling, the most profound one was fear. I wanted so hard not to feel that way. [If I put fear out into the universe, it would be.] I was scared to death that he would fail himself, the consequences of that would be harsh and severe. If he got arrested for anything, he would violate probation, which could send him back to prison for up to seven years.

I parked the car, and when I heard the loud whistle of the train blow, I got out of the car and walked around to the other side and leaned against it. I, again, was anxious, as the train came into sight and began pulling up. It came to a stop and people poured out of it. Joey and I saw each other at the very same moment, and as he walked faster, I walked towards him. We gave each other a great big hug. My baby boy was free from jail!

His first question was where were his brothers? I told him that we would go surprise them. When I thought about it, I realized not one of them had mentioned this morning about his coming home today. I assumed that the weekend had relieved them of any anticipating emotions they would have of their brother's return.

He didn't have that much stuff with him, and when I asked him where everything was, he said he didn't want to bring anything except his letters and a few books, one of them being the Bible; he gave all his stuff away. I couldn't say I blamed him.

It was just about time for A.J. to be released from school, so we got in the car and headed over there. During the drive Joey was asking questions about the boys, the neighbors, his friends. While he was talking, I was thinking it didn't seem like he was gone for nine months, however, he perhaps probably felt as if he were gone for nine years.

Joey came with me to the entrance of the school for A.J. and when A.J. saw me his face lit up as it always does. Then he saw Joey and his big brown eyes grew even bigger and his smile stretched widely across his face. He was incredibly excited to see his big brother and Joey was just as excited to see him. A.J. ran to him, screaming his name. It was a very sweet moment.

We went back to the house to wait for Anthony to get home from school. I was a little nervous knowing Anthony did not have a good relationship with Joey. Anthony I understood was not going to be capable of putting things behind him so easily. I hadn't had a private moment to speak with Anthony about Joey staying with us over the weekend and suddenly regretted it. I almost felt like I was sacrificing one child's happiness for another. Though that was not the case, it was certainly how I felt. I hoped that if Joey stayed on the right path Anthony would build trust in his brother and they could have that relationship that they both deserved to have.

I could see Anthony's bus pull up from the kitchen window and I felt a slight knot in my stomach. He came in and as usual said, "Hi, Mom." As soon as he saw Joey standing there, his face changed. It was an odd look. Not one of joy but not disgust either. He almost politely forced himself to smile. He was happy to see him because he was his brother but I don't think he was happy to see him here in our kitchen, in our house, in his space. Joey gave him a big bear hug and Anthony smiled and laughed. Joey asked him all kinds of questions about his life, school, and how he enjoyed his mini-vacation. They seemed to be having a normal conversation and I wished this was how it always was, how it always could be, like a normal family.

It was their father's night to have the boys, but I called and said I wanted to take them out to dinner. He understood and actually told me he would join us if he could get out of work early enough.

I was upstairs getting ready for dinner when Anthony came to me in the first private moment he could have with me. He asked me directly if Joey was going to stay with us. I felt my heart sink. I knew for him to ask me, it was on his mind and a concern for him. I looked at him and told him that I wanted to be honest with him and that I thought it might be a good idea if we gave him a second chance. Anthony immediately replied, "A second chance? Hasn't he had a few of those already?" I held his hands and explained to him that as much as he knew I loved him, I loved

Joey also, and that he had spent nine months in jail and maybe that would be a hard lesson learned for Joey and a change for the better. He rolled his eyes, he pierced his lips. I couldn't blame him. I asked him to try; that's all I could ask. I held him close and promised him that the first time Joey slipped up he would have to leave. He just looked at me for a moment and I held him close and kissed his forehead with a kiss of reassurance.

Chapter Nineteen

Having Joey back home was going to be an adjustment for all of us. In spite of being hopeful that we could function as a normal family functioned, I had to be direct with him regarding the rules. We were going to move forward, not go backwards. I knew I had to be flexible since he was twenty-one now, however, if he wasn't going to respect the rules he could reside someplace else.

I expected him to get a job or go to school and in return would give him his old room back. I expected him to ask if he wanted anything, not to take it upon himself to just take it. I expected him to treat his brothers kindly and with respect. There would be no hitting, screaming, or cursing at them.

I anticipated that he would connect with some of his old friends, so I made it very clear to him that this is it, if he violated the rules and expectations of this house, just like his probation there would be consequences and they would be harsh. The end result would be he would not live here anymore, especially since Anthony had reluctantly lost his faith in me that all would be fine and Joey would make a complete change in the direction his life was going. I believed Anthony's intuition was probably correct, because deep down I felt the same as he but as a mom I had to have faith and do all I could do for my child until I couldn't do any more.'

For a couple of weeks Joey searched for work. I would ask him how the job hunt was going and he would reply something like, "It's hard to find a job with a felony." I tried to understand his frustration but I also believed he could have searched with more vigilance; the less you searched the less your chances were of actually finding work. I tried explaining to him how important it was that he remained positive, that the emotional aspect of repeatedly being rejected would weigh heavily on him but he would need to find the inner strength to push forward.

He apparently managed to get back together with his ex-girlfriend Kima. He met her when she was one month pregnant by; allegedly, a married man who left when he found out she was going to have the baby.

There was a day early in their relationship when she was quite a few months pregnant and he and I were having a conversation about his behavior that turned into a brutal argument. He had put a hole in the wall and broke a rod iron candle holder of mine. He ended by kicking the side of my car. She was there, outside, sitting in her car waiting for him. I walked over to her, looked at her, and told her, "Remember these words: I'm his mother and this is how he treats me. How do you think he is going to treat you and your child?" She just looked at me. She couldn't speak because the possibility that there might be any truth to my words startled her. He got in her car and they drove away.

I wondered if she would keep him grounded and off the streets. I thought that after being locked up and getting a second chance with Kima and the baby it would motivate him to want a nice life, settle down and be a family man. I was very proud of Kima. She had finished getting her medical training while he was incarcerated and found work in a medical office. She was doing beautifully raising Sequoia,, who was precious, but in my heart of hearts, I knew Joey at this moment in time was not ready to be anyone's father, and though he loved them, sometimes love was not enough.

June had passed and Joey finally landed a job. It was a temp within the DOT but it was a job. His duties would vary from day to day. He might be clipping tree branches that hung over the streets or helping to keep the parks clean, maybe painting, or driving around the City picking up orange drums that were used to block off roads or for road work. It was a great job with great hours. He went in at seven and was done by two. It was a job where he could possibly get his foot in the door for a permanent position and make a nice future for himself.

I felt like things were finally falling into place. Over the next month and a half things were great. I enjoyed going home from work. I looked forward to making nice dinners and having everyone here, the boys, Joey, Kima, and Sequoia. We packed picnics on weekends and went to the beach. It felt like a complete family for the first time in a long time. The boys loved that their big brother played video games with them and truly enjoyed when we were all together in the backyard having a barbecue.

In the early morning of summer I loved to sit on the patio listening to the birds delicately chirp. It brought peace to my heart. I would sip on my coffee and have an enormous feeling of relief.

I would sit and quietly talk with God, thanking him for giving me back my son. I had forgotten how sweet and funny Joey could actually be. It had been many years since I had seen him this happy and many years since this family had functioned in a normal healthy manner. Joey was finally on the right path. I thanked God for Joey getting up every morning without hesitation to go to work. I was grateful for how he was interacting with his brothers. I had never seen this side of him.

Joey had discovered the joy he had within himself. He and his friends met at the pool when everyone got off work. On weekends they would go out to Long Island to the beach and at night experience the City and all it had to offer young people. It was delightful to see him being a normal 21 year old and living his life in a positive manner. I thanked the Lord for giving me the strength and the faith to give my child one more chance.

Since he was incarcerated for his 21st birthday, I decided to throw him a belated surprise party. At this point he had reached that milestone deservingly so and I thought it would make him feel proud and also thankful for everything he had.

I planned the party for August 2d 2009. I was taking great pride and pleasure in planning it. It was the first opportunity in a while for me to do something special for him. I was thankful to have a chance to re-create his birthday and make it as it should have been if he hadn't been incarcerated for it. I planned the appetizers, the entrées, and the desserts. The cake would have his picture on it from when he turned one. There would be a champagne toast, cream puffs, and a fountain of chocolate for dipping treats. There would be music and everyone would feel the sound of a joyous tune playing from my household.

It was mid July when Joey decided to quit his job. He told me he felt belittled by some of the jobs they were asking him to do, such as wash police cars. I was trying to be understanding and thought it was more a matter of ego. I thought he should have found another job before quitting, but it was done, and I explained that he did have to actively search for another job.

My fear was that idle time would lead to an uneasiness that would manifest itself in negative behaviors again.

Chapter Twenty

August 2d I awoke to the sound of rain. It was pouring so hard that it was making clinking sounds against the gutters that hung off the edge of the roof. Normally there is such a peaceful feeling when listening to the rain. I didn't know why, but it brought me comfort.

I lay there in bed thinking how special the day was going to be for Joey. He was going to be so surprised that we were celebrating his 21st birthday.

I wanted this party to be grand, so I also thought of all the food I had been preparing. I needed to make sure that I left nothing out. I was having shrimp cocktail, mussels marinara, crawfish, anti-pasta, stuffed mushrooms, teriyaki wings, homemade macaroni and cheese, baked ziti, sausage and peppers, and jambalaya. Everything was homemade and made with love. I thought that all I really needed to do as far as the food went was to prepare the fish and the jambalaya.

I stood up and went over to the window to open it. The rain sounded even louder as it came down with such force. There was an old pine tree that hung over the window where I was standing. Its branches protected me from getting wet. I looked out onto the backyard and thought there was so much I needed to do out there and the yard was soaked. I went over to turn the TV on to listen to the weather. I was hoping Sam Champion was on, as he was the only weatherman I trusted, well the cutest one anyway. I was somewhat panicking that the rain wouldn't stop but I had to believe that it would. This day was very special not just for Joey but for me as well. I'd waited twenty-one years to celebrate my son entering adult-hood. I've waited many years just to celebrate anything positive with him that was about him with our family and friends.

The weather forecast stated it would clear up by the mid afternoon. I felt an immense relief or at least hope because as I looked out the window it surely didn't look like it would stop anytime soon. I was thankful that I had planned for an evening party so everyone was not expected until then, which gave me ample time to set up the backyard.

I went to make coffee and Joey came downstairs, taunting me that I couldn't have a party in this weather. He thought it was a summer barbecue because I was thinking that if he knew it was for him he surely would have a different perception and would be saying the opposite. I told him the weatherman said it would stop around two. Joey looked at me and said, "This isn't stopping, Ma."

"Aren't you going somewhere with your friends today?" I asked him. Little did he know, his friends were in on it, and I also thought to myself that everything was under control… well, everything but the weather.

The phone was ringing throughout the morning with people wanting to know if I was cancelling, but I told them the party was on. I would answer, "Yes of course," trying to come across as if I weren't remotely the slightest bit panicky and really tried to sound as if I had complete faith in Sam Champion.

As I was making the jambalaya, I realized Joey was not leaving fast enough. I needed him to leave so I could run to the store and purchase last-minute things that I could not buy, like balloons, that would give up the party was for him. I looked out the window to see his friend pulling up and thought aloud, thank God, he must have read my mind.

As Joey was leaving, he kissed me goodbye and said, "You still having this thing, Ma?"

"Yes, Joey I'll see you a little later and don't be later than five because your grandmother will want to see you."

"Yep," he answered, as he was halfway out the door.

As I watched them walk to his friend's car I thought of the many different realms of emotions that I had experienced over the past few years that were indescribable. From the time Joey was about fourteen or fifteen I felt frustration, and as he grew older I felt an immense sadness from inside that I had no control or was quickly losing control. The more I tried, the more oppositional he became. On glimmers of hope when there would be little pieces of normalcy, all I wanted was to embrace him and hold on to him so tightly that he would not re-enter the ugly world outside. I had had moments where I would have burst at the seams with faith that he would change his life and I had had insecure moments of doubt, expecting what I knew to be.

I thought back to many years ago when I met a man whose humor was addicting, whose looks were tantalizing. I was mesmerized by him and he could do no wrong. By the time I realized there was a problem, because I couldn't see it, even though I knew it, the drinking, the drugging, the stealing, it was too late, I had married the devil.

I thought I could change him; I couldn't. I thought he would stop abusing drugs and alcohol for me; he didn't. He got worse and my life became a bad dream and he was the monster in my nightmare. I didn't even leave him when he nearly broke my nose, or the time he smashed my head into the car door repeatedly but when things got to the point where Joey was being affected emotionally it was past time to leave. I could only hope that the time that he was in our life would not have a long-term effect on Joey.

Once we split up and he was gone, it was not too difficult for me to put our lives back on track. I had great friends who were incredibly supportive. Enough time had passed where the fear of my husband coming back into our lives didn't consume my daily thoughts anymore, until the day when I ran home on a break from work and found an intruder in my closet, I'll never forget the day when I saw the silhouette of a man pressed up against the side of the wall.

Without looking to see his face in the darkness, I knew it was him, and as my heart dropped, I felt the strength in my legs leading me, carrying me fast out of the closet.

I hoped those brief moments of insecurities I had of my son failing were only minute moments of memories from a past that I have tried to erase from my mind. I needed to concentrate on the present and not worry about something that might never be. I needed to believe and help guide my son to be focused and ready to face his future with optimism, humility, and appreciation for the second chance he had in his young life.

Today was a day to celebrate so after Joey left I went and bought balloons that read, "Happy 21st Birthday," I ran to get ice and headed home to decorate. As I was driving, I looked at the sky and begged God for it to stop raining. It was almost as if the rain knew how special this day was. The rain stopped, the clouds were parting, and the sun was beginning to shed its light on us. I knew at that moment that all would be well.

I was relieved that my mother and a few girlfriends came early. They must have known I would definitely need a few extra hands. I draped the outside tables in linens. I filled the coolers with ice and filled them to the brim with different beverages. I set up the dessert table with the chocolate fountain and champagne glasses. I put six balloons in each table secured by balloon weights. I hung simple clear lights from tree to tree and put white candles all around so when the sun went down after blissfully blessing us with its presence the ambiance would continue to embrace us throughout the evening into the night. I placed red and white wine on the tables.

Everything was set up. Kima was there with the baby, our friends and family had arrived, the music was playing, the appetizers were out, and all we needed was Joey to show up. I called his friend to let him know we were ready and to call me when they were almost here. When he called we all gathered on the patio, and when he walked back there, we all screamed, "Surprise!"

It was a fantastic moment. I watched him as he went around shaking hands with the men and hugging the women, kissing them on the cheek. I could see the joy in his face as he felt accepted and loved unconditionally by everyone there. He felt there was no judgment for past mistakes. He knew that this was all for him. As the late afternoon moved into the evening, we all ate and we drank and we laughed. And we ate, and we drank, and we laughed. We all celebrated his 21st birthday.

As the evening moved into the night, we continued to celebrate. A friend's husband brought in a huge speaker that was about to shake the entire city of Peekskill with sounds of what should be karaoke. My girlfriend Julia was the first to break the ice to get on the mic and belt out her vocals across the entire neighborhood. When she was done, everyone was clapping and whistling. Her energy was infectious, and as soon as she put the mic down everyone, including Joey and his friends, was ready to sing and share their vocal talents. It was great to see everyone, young and younger, having an amazing time.

I put 21 candles on the cake and an extra one for good luck. The boys' dad carried it out and we all sang the "happy birthday" song to him. He blew out the candles and we clapped and cheered for him. I poured champagne into glasses and we all gathered and made a toast to Joey. He hugged me and said, "Thanks, Mom." It wasn't what he said to me, it was how he said it, with appreciation. I felt so proud. I felt my son's soul had returned and I had him back.

Chapter Twenty-One

The few weeks that followed the party, continued to be good for us. It had been three months since Joey had been home from jail and we were all pretty much settled in and adjusted to his living with us. Though the summer was coming to an end, we were spending every minute together.

The last weeks of summer were rather chilly and our days at the beach ended, but we were still able to cook out and enjoy the summer evenings together building fires and toasting marshmallows. Kima would always ask Joey if I were cooking. Sometimes I wouldn't plan on it but because she would ask I would cook just so she could come over with the baby and I could spend time with the two of them.

Going into September, Joey still hadn't found any work and I hadn't pushed the issue because I knew this was the last summer for him before it was time for him to grow up and then be working every summer for the rest of his life. He had also registered and applied for financial aid for a heating and air conditioning course and upon completion he would have a certificate and be able to obtain work in that field.

I found myself feeling so proud of him which I hadn't felt in quite a while. When other people expressed joy over their children, of course, I am happy for them, but secretly I wished so desperately that I could feel that same joy about my child. What it must feel like to hold no shame or embarrassment, nothing bitter, just sweet, pleasant thoughts of a child who has grown to be a kind, respectful human being not just to others, but to his own self. How important it is for each of us to respect ourselves. It's one of the many important things we can teach our children.

Anthony's birthday was approaching and he was turning sixteen, which was a special one. Every kid waits anxiously for that birthday so they can go get their permit. I thought I would have a small party for him, which would be another excuse for me to embrace everyone with food and laughter in celebration of him.

When his birthday finally approached it was a rather warm night so we were able to be outside in the backyard. The teenagers were hanging outside in the gazebo and the adults were, of course, sitting around the table talking.

I had gone inside to get a bottle of wine, where I met Kima arriving with the baby. She always had Sequoia dressed so adorably. She told her to show me the beautiful delicate new gold necklace Joey had bought for her. She made a simple statement, as she was showing me, that there was a matching bracelet but that she already lost it. I said, "Very pretty. When did Joey buy that for you?"

Her mommy answered for her, "Two days ago."

I kissed the baby and told her the necklace was as pretty as she was and then told Kima to take her outside with everyone else and I would be there in a minute.

Sometimes things happen for a reason. Sometimes you know something before you know it. Sometimes you will hear something and not be sure what it quite means but it will stay with you in the back of your head and in the bottom of your gut. When it is ready to be known it will rise inside of you and suddenly it will make you aware.

My instinct in that very 1/100 of a second told me something was off. I wasn't sure what it was, but I was sure it would make itself known when it was ready or when I was ready to face it, even if it may be a truth. He had quit his job quite a while ago, so I knew he had no money, which is why I asked her when he bought it, so as not to jump to conclusions. I was hoping she would say, a while ago, and that the baby is only wearing it now. When she answered" two days ago," it confirmed the instinct that fed my curiosity.

I wasn't going to interrogate Joey that night or any other night for that matter, but I was going to watch and pay attention. I had been unaware or unconscious the past few weeks while basking in the joy and happiness as my immediate family had been reunited together with love, so much that it had blinded me.

I got the wine and returned outside to join everyone. I introduced Kima and Sequoia to a few people they didn't know and we all engaged in great conversation. I brought out the cake and coffee and we all enjoyed Anthony's birthday. Joey had sat down near me for a few minutes and I casually mentioned to him the gold necklace he bought for the baby was beautiful and how unfortunate it was that she lost the matching bracelet. He looked at me maybe for 1/100 of a second, long enough for him to know something was off but he wasn't quite sure what it was. But he knew when I knew, he would know. He then responded, "You saw it?"

"Of course, Kima showed it to me. Very nice," I replied with a slight tone only my sons would pick up on. He just looked at me, not quite sure.

A conscious state is where I needed to be at all times. All parents need to be there no matter how much they love and trust their children. We get lost in the unconditional love we have for our children and then the clarity we need to guide them dissipates. I knew I could not afford that loss, we as a society could not afford that loss. By denying to ourselves what we know is the truth that is impacting our children, how are we helping them? We are denying them the future they deserve, the future we dreamt for them while they were still in the womb. We are inhibiting them and stunting their growth into productive adults.

I needed to be, we all need to be, aware, aware of what our children are doing and who they are doing it with. If not, there would be many sleepless nights and many tears shed. Violence, gangs, alcohol, drugs, such as cocaine, crack, speed, heroine, your mother's valium, your father's pain medicine, even the can of paint or the bottle of glue or the can of whipped cream that sits in the refrigerator are poisons that are destroying our youth.

We needed to be aware of the smallest things that did not seem right or fit into the norm of how we know our children.

I knew my child. I knew something was wrong. I knew in 1/100 of a split second. And now I was going to pay attention, and I was aware, and I was conscious, and I hoped I was wrong.

Chapter Twenty-Two

When I was sleeping later that night I woke up to the sound of Joey's bedroom door opening. I heard him go down the stairs and then I heard the front door open. I looked at the clock and it was shortly after two in the morning. I was wondering what he was doing and where he was going at this hour of the morning when just a few minutes had gone by and I heard him come back in and go to his room, where he shut the door and stayed in his room for the rest of the night. I drifted off to sleep wondering about my son. Something felt off to me. I replayed conversations, events, the gold necklace, new clothes, and no job. I fell asleep.

The week had gone by and on Friday night the two younger boys and I went to my dear friends' Janna and Greg's, who were having a barbecue. We were there for maybe an hour when my cell phone was ringing. It was Joey. "Mom, where are you? What are you doing? Is Anthony with you?" There was a strange tone to his voice, but I told him we were down the street at Janna's and asked him if he wanted to join us. He didn't want to, but I told him that if he changed his mind he knew where we were.

About fifteen minutes went by and he was calling again. He was asking me if I was going to be there and I told him to just come down and that he didn't have to stay if he didn't want to but he should come and eat and that it would be nice if he could hang out with us for a while. He agreed and before I knew it, he was joining us.

When he came into the backyard he was greeting everyone, but when he looked at me his eyes looked strange, there was distance in them, a blank look that I have seen before. He sat down and immediately asked me where Anthony was. I told him he was inside but I wanted Joey to stay outside with us for a while, the reason being I could feel something was off and I knew if I watched him I would most likely pick up on what it was.

He sat next to me on a lawn chair and was oddly quiet. I asked him if he was okay, and even though he was telling me he was fine, I knew he was not. I asked him if he wanted to eat, which he did, so I made him a plate. As he bit into his burger he asked me again where his brother Anthony was. "I told you he's inside. Why are you so concerned with where he is?" He said he was just asking, but I knew there was more to this. He finished eating and sat there for a few moments. I could sense the edginess that was trying to escape him. He got up to put his paper plate in the garbage, came back, and said he was going inside. I nodded my head in acknowledgement to him and even though I was engaged in conversation I was aware and knew I needed to go inside to let him know I was watching him without letting everyone else know I needed to watch my adult child.

      I allowed ten minutes to go by before I said I needed to go in to use the bathroom. The older kids were in the boys' bedroom playing video games. I poked my head in to see if anyone needed anything; no one did. I asked my boys Joey and Anthony if they were okay, if they wanted anything else to eat, and they both said they were fine. I went back outside feeling relieved, wondering if maybe I was overreacting. I was wondering if I was always going to be this way, not trusting my child, wondering if every time he was having a bad day I would be suspicious that it was something more than just that.

I sat down with everyone at the picnic table and joined back in the conversation. We were having a good laugh when one of the girls came running out screaming that Joey was beating up Anthony. She was yelling that he was punching him. The conversation stopped as we all were processing what she was saying. I jumped up and ran towards the house. She was screaming to "hurry up" over and over again until I got to the door. I ran into the house and ran to the other end of the house, to the boys' bedroom. Anthony was crying and yelling with such anger in his voice how much he hated him. Greg was behind me and he was asking the boys what happened. Everyone was talking at once and finally Greg's son explained that Joey had said out of the blue that he messed his life up. He said they all just looked at him, not sure if he was going to continue to speak. With that, Joey looked at Anthony, who made a face at him and rolled his eyes as if he cared about what Joey had to say, and with that, Joey had jumped on Anthony and had started hitting him.

I ran to the front door to see if Joey was still around but he was not. I went back to Anthony who was sitting on the bed wiping his tears away. I walked over to him and gave him a hug. He was hurt and he was angry. He was let down once again after trying to let his brother in. It had taken him almost the entire summer to rebuild the trust he had lost in Joey, to be able to sit in the same room with him, to interact with him. It was beyond obvious that every time Joey would enter a space where Anthony was, Anthony would casually exit the room.

As much as I felt us growing as a family and working through our issues, as much as we were working towards functioning as a healthy family unit, Anthony always had reservations. I felt so bad for him. When he hurts, I hurt. I let him be with his friends to talk and I went outside to get some air and to talk with Janna and Greg about what happened. I was feeling humiliated once again at Joey's behavior.

I had seen the emptiness in Joey's eyes. I had felt the anxiousness riveting within him as he sat there eating his burger. Why I didn't do something, I asked myself. I have seen that look before and I knew deep within me that the rage that lurked within was going to find a way to overcome Joey, it was going to take control of him, and the demons that were deep inside of him, waiting patiently, were going to lash out at the innocent child that was always the target of that rage. The rage needed to be fed. Too much time had gone by and it needed to be fed.

I was so angry at Joey, at myself. I was disappointed. I was hurt and confused that Joey would strike out at Anthony again. I thought we had made strides and thought we were moving forward. I had been in denial. I had wanted things to be normal and change so much that I just convinced myself that they had. Joey had not changed; I only wanted so badly to believe he had, that I could not see the truth.

He didn't come home that night. I didn't call him either. He knew he was wrong, so he avoided me the next day as well. As nighttime came, I tried to sleep, but I would drift in and out of consciousness because my mind was in such turmoil trying to figure out what was going on with him that it would not allow me to sleep, so, instead, I lay in bed heavy in thought.

I must have finally dozed off at some point as I woke up to the sound of the front door squeaking as it was being slowly closed. I realized Joey was trying to sneak in after believing that I had fallen asleep. I heard him coming up the stairs and trying to walk softly down the hall to his room. I shut my eyes, knowing I was too tired to argue with him now. I felt them getting heavier and heavier with a sense of relief that he was home.

All of a sudden I heard him coming back up the hall and going down the stairs, and out the front door. Instantly my body jolted awake and I jumped out of bed and ran to the other side of the house to look out his bedroom window, which overlooked the front yard. In the dark I stood in his room, and peeking out through the curtain looking out into the blackness of night, I saw the shadow of a man walking down the sidewalk. As his body reached the streetlight I could tell it was definitely Joey in shorts and flip flops, not dressed to go anywhere, yet he was going around the corner.

I went back to my bedroom and wondered what he was doing in the middle of the night. Only a few moments had passed when I heard the front door open and he was back again.

The next morning I was exhausted from not sleeping but managed to get myself up for work. As I was getting ready to leave the house, Joey had gone down the stairs in the same shorts and flip-flops and gone out again. I was looking out the kitchen window as he ran around the corner.

I got the boys in the car to drop them off at school. As I came around the corner, I could see down the street that Joey was talking to someone in a shiny baby blue SUV. When he turned his head and saw my car, his arm rescinded from the car window and it seemed the person he was talking to quickly wanted to leave the area.

As I passed him, our eyes met. I wanted to catch up to the SUV, which I did at the stop sign. I was surprised to see a woman in her late thirties behind the wheel. I'd never seen her before and wondered why she was meeting my son around the corner. My instincts were screaming at me that I already knew.

Chapter Twenty-Three

I was restless at work that day, and it seemed endless. I wanted so desperately to get home. I had a problem, a serious problem, which my instincts told me were worse than anything I could ever have imagined, and I prayed for strength and guidance.

On my drive home, of course my thoughts dwelled on Joey. I wondered what was going on with him, what happened to him. All day, I could only think of Joey going in and out of the house for moments at a time. I knew and could sense so strongly that he was selling drugs. Was there a moment he made a conscious decision to choose this path? I wasn't going to deny it to myself anymore. I knew what he was doing. I think I knew the night Sequoia showed me her necklace. At what moment did he decide to quit on himself?

When I was finally able to get the boys from school and get home, Joey was not there and I felt relieved. I actually anticipated such, being I'm sure he realized I knew something was going on that he knew I would not be happy about.

I put my bag down, the boys scattered, one upstairs to his video game, the other to the refrigerator. I put the water on for a cup of tea and sorted through the mail. When my tea was ready, I took it upstairs with me to my room to change my clothes from work and thought I would read for a little while or write in my journal before I started dinner. I needed some time to relax my mind and get my thoughts together.

Some time had passed by and my tea got cold. I started to go downstairs to heat it up but, instead, I found myself going into Joey's room. I walked over to his night table and set my tea down on it. I ran my fingers across a few papers and objects that were on the lower shelf. A couple of the papers fell off the shelf onto the carpet. I started to pick them up and as my eyes focused there were little itty-bitty pieces of plastic. I held one up and it looked like a little mini Ziploc bag. I stood up and just stared at the floor. With the truth slapping me in the face, I became disorientated.

I needed to go heat up my tea, so I went downstairs and as it was heating up in the microwave I was trying to process what I had seen, what I was thinking, and what I was feeling. As I stood in front of the microwave in silence, in realization that those bags were new and unused, I knew they were for distribution of something. I found myself stepping on a chair and opening cupboard doors to run my hand across the top shelves of cabinets I could reach. The buzzer sound went off on the microwave to let me know my tea was done, but I continued to open up other cabinets, looking in bowls, cups, and containers I no longer use.

      A memory popped into my head about a time when before he went off to jail on a warrant he had stayed with my mother for a little while. Some weeks had passed after he was incarcerated when my mother was cleaning and getting rid of some things. She had pulled out an old VCR from the entertainment center in her bedroom and behind it was a big bag of marijuana that Joey had hidden.

I was dumbfounded that he would bring and hide this in her house right under her nose; it was unfathomable to me. Assuming people are habitual I was curious if he had put something right under my nose, something anyplace in the house that he thought I would not be smart enough to find. The boys were home and I didn't want them knowing anything, so I decided to keep this to myself until I figured out how to handle it.

The next day was a half day at school and my mother was coming to watch the boys so I wouldn't have to leave work early which I truly appreciated. I slowly opened Joey's bedroom door to see if he had come home during the night while I was asleep and he had. I closed the door gently.

When I came home my mother met me at the door and we spoke briefly because she, herself, had to get to the hospital to work that night. She just said the boys were fine and Joey was there for most the day but left a little while ago. Of course, he did, I thought to myself. I gave her hugs and kisses and then she left.

I threw my bag on the stairs and went into the kitchen to get a bottle of water. I felt extremely hungry, so I decided I wanted to make an early dinner. After I prepared everything, I bent down to get the foil from the bottom drawer to cover the food and there, before my eyes, on the kitchen floor, was a little piece of somewhat-twisted plastic. I picked it up and drew it closer. I held it even a bit closer, because I couldn't tell if something was in it or if it was just the plastic.

As I delicately was pulling the plastic apart, I carefully opened it. It appeared to have the consistency of soap but was quite small, maybe the size of a chocolate chip divided into quarters. I knew what it was. I knew how it got on the kitchen floor. I stood there silenced. My words were taken from me, my thoughts were taken from me; I just stood there.

I wrapped it back up and stuffed it into my pocket in case one of the boys entered the kitchen. I stood there leaning against the counter, frozen. Reality was slapping me even harder in the face. I held my hands over my mouth and nose. I thought of all the what if's, and no conclusion was a good one, except the fact that I had found it on the floor and no one else had.

There was absolutely no logical reason for a piece of crack cocaine to be sitting on the kitchen floor. It was as if God himself had pulled it out of Joey's pocket and dropped it on the floor so I would be able to see it, so my eyes would be forced open and I would finally realize the truth of what was going on. It was confirmation of something I only thought but could not prove, those thoughts that I kept in the back of my head, unable to bring forth. Now it was here in my face, where I would bend over to get the foil from the bottom drawer, and sitting on the kitchen floor was not just a piece of crack but a little piece of the truth.

I called my mother at work knowing she couldn't talk if anyone was around, but I needed to talk to her. I explained what happened and how I found it.

She said to me, "He wasn't in the kitchen."

With surprise, I asked her, "What?"

"Sheila, he never came into the kitchen the whole time I was there."

I couldn't believe the denial. "Well, Ma I don't do drugs, so it's certainly not my crack on the floor! I have to go." I abruptly ended the call.

I called my son on impulse because now I was raging mad, but I ended the call before he answered. I needed to get calm, I needed to think. Then I called again, and when he answered the phone, I said, "We need to talk."

"About what?"

"Joey, I found a piece of crack on the kitchen floor. You have two options: one, you can go to a long-term rehab, or you can leave my house."

"Okay."

"(Okay) what? I waited for answer and when there was none I asked again, what is your choice?"

This time he abruptly ended the call on me. I stood there boiling in my anger. The anger caused by my mother's denial, my son's rudeness, my son's addiction.

I walked up the stairs slowly to Joey's room. I lay on his bed and stared at the pictures of him and some friends as they were growing up. I turned my head and looked at the Bible that sat on the table next to his bed, rosary beads hung on the other wall, and I was surprised at all the religious items.

I wanted to rip through my son's room. I sat there replaying the last two weeks in my mind and the dramatic change in Joey that was rapidly occurring right in front of me. I sat there, looking around the room, scanning the dresser and all the drawers, the shelf on the wall, the box that sat next to his closet. I got up and went over to his dresser and found myself opening up each drawer. In one, there were quite a few receipts from different stores with recent dates. I wondered where he got the money to buy all this stuff. I knew where he was getting the money. I took everything out of the dresser and I ran my hand underneath each drawer. I don't know why, I never in a million years, ever thought of doing such a thing. I thought maybe it was ridiculous and I watched too many movies. But I did, and to my ambiguous amazement, my fingers touched something and when I gently pulled it out, there were two twenties being held between the wood frame and the bottom of the drawer.

      I sat on the carpet thinking and then looked over at his bed and under the bed. I was going to go through every article of clothing and every item he owned. I was going to search every inch of his room. There were sneakers and boots under the bed and I ran my fingers through each shoe but found nothing.

I stood up and went to his closet and searched in and out of each pocket in each shirt, each jacket, and every pair of pants. All my hand came across was bits and pieces of papers but then I found something else. I pulled it out of a pocket that was on the inside panel of a coat. I looked down into the palm of my hand and in it was a second little piece of soap-like substance wrapped in plastic.

I felt my heart sink into my chest. I suddenly felt rage, an intense rage that surged quickly through my body. I never felt this before. I needed to breathe and get control of my emotions that were starting to run loose. I wanted to get in my car and find him. I wanted to get something solid and big and hard and when I found him I wanted to kick his ass with it wherever I found him. I wanted to drop him to his knees wherever he stood. I was beyond anger crying tears of disappointment, failure, and frustration. I had failed my son.

I pushed through my tears and my anger and I searched for more. I knew there had to be more. I didn't know why it would matter. I had found enough to know that my son was in trouble. I had found a Ziploc bag stuffed with dozens and dozens of little mini Ziploc bags like the ones I found before. I continued to search through the rest of his things, even his socks and CD cases and baseball card albums. In another pocket of a shirt I found two more pieces of crack.

I called him and left a message since he would not answer his phone. I simply stated, "I found a few more pieces of crack in your things. Don't bother coming home."

I looked around at the clothes on his bed and the clothes on his floor that I had ripped from the hangers in his closet. His room was wrecked and when I turned around both boys were standing in the doorway watching me. When our eyes met they could see the immense sadness in me. Anthony asked me what I was doing with Joey's stuff and I wasn't quite sure how to answer him. I stood there for a moment then reminded him of the promise to him that if Joey ever started to retract back to his old ways that he would have to leave...It was time for him to leave.

Chapter Twenty-Four

A week and a day went by and I had not heard from Joey since I had given him an ultimatum. He hadn't even come to retrieve any of his belongings. I assumed he knew I was done and he was embarrassed. Eventually we would have to face what was in front of us. Eventually he would call because he would have to face what was in front of him.

The following Tuesday night his girlfriend, Kima, had called to ask if she could come by and get a coat for him. It was rather late, about twenty to ten, but I told her she could since it was getting cold out. Not even five minutes had passed when A.J. said there was a man at the door. I was confused but thought maybe she sent someone for the coat.

I went to the door and when I saw a middle-aged man standing there I was a bit taken aback. I realized the man looked familiar. He lived here in the same complex and his daughter Carla had gone to the senior prom with Joey. I thought it was odd he was standing at my door. I said hello to him and he just stood there looking at me. He was looking at me as though I should have something to tell him.

I finally said, "Is everything okay?"

"My daughter told me to come to your house."

I replied to him that "Kima just called me," assuming that maybe Joey asked Carla to go get the coat for him. He looked extremely confused. I said to him, "I'm not sure what you are talking about. Why did your daughter tell you to come here? Was it for a coat for Joey?"

"I don't know. My daughter called me and was whispering into the phone to (go to the boys) house that I went to the prom with?" We both stood there staring at each other like the other should know what was going on yet we were both very confused and neither one of us knew what was going on.

His cell phone rang, breaking the awkwardness and he waved his hand to me to let me know it was his daughter on the other end of the phone. I whispered to him to let me speak with her. He handed me the phone and I asked her what was going on. She started saying that she and Joey had gone to a department store and the police arrested her for shoplifting. They wanted Joey too but he had run. Before I could respond a state trooper got on the phone. He asked me if I knew where my son was and, if I heard from him would I tell him, to give them a call. I gave the phone back to Carla's father, feeling even more confused.

I had no idea where Joey was but thought I could safely assume he was with Kima at that moment. All of a sudden I remembered that Kima had never come for the coat. Maybe she had come and saw this man at the front door and not knowing who he was decided to not get the coat. I thought about Joey being on probation and that if he got arrested for shoplifting he would have a violation charge as well. The only reason I didn't call her to find out why she didn't come over or if she knew what was going on was because of the baby; it was late and Sequoia might be sleeping.

I went to work the following day. I was normally off on Wednesdays but I had a client that could only make it in on that day, so I went in for her. I was with her for over an hour and a half and had maybe another twenty minutes to go until I finished her hair when my cell phone rang. I could see on the Caller ID that it was my middle son's godmother, Karen.

"Hey Karen, I'm with a client right now. I'm almost done with her hair. Can I call you back in a little while?"

"Sheila, the police are looking for Joey," she said, her voice calm to keep me calm she continued, "My grandmother just heard it on the scanner. Sheila, there are police dogs and a helicopter outside the building. There are police all over the place." I was trying to absorb what she was saying. I was trying to process the words "police" "dogs" and "helicopter". I was trying to process that the building she was talking about was the building Joey's grandmother lived at.

"What?" The tone and slight elevation in my voice sounded so alarming that my girlfriends at work immediately knew that something was wrong.

My phone beeped to signal there was another call coming in. I told her to hold on.

"Mom! Mom!" He was out of breath.

"Joey, what is going on? What is happening?"

"Oh my God Mom!" I could hear the fear in his voice. My eyes instantaneously started to swell with tears. I knew my son was in trouble and I couldn't help him.

I knew it was true what Karen had just told me. My brain was scrambling to understand the severity of a helicopter search. I reached for the wall behind me to help me get my balance, because I was suddenly feeling lightheaded and dizzy.

He was talking to me as he was running and he was breathing heavy. "Mom, I didn't do anything! They aimed a gun at me and told me if I moved they would shoot!"

"Oh, my God! What? Why?"

"I didn't do anything, Ma!"

In a soft voice, almost not wanting to hear the truth, I asked him, "Joey, is there a helicopter looking for you?"

"Yeah, but they are crazy! I didn't do anything."

I suddenly felt as though I had stopped breathing. My legs were so weak they couldn't hold me up and I fell to the floor on my knees, sobbing into the phone, "Oh, my God. What did you do? What did you do?" I cried to him. I could hear dogs barking in the background. I thought I was going to pass out.

"Mom, the dogs are after me. I'm not sticking around here."

Then there was a click, and I screamed into the phone, "Joey!" I laid on the floor repeatedly crying out his name and I got no answer. I was crying so hard I started to hyperventilate. I was crying so hard I didn't even realize my girlfriends in the salon were crying.

My client had a look of shock on her face. Julia and Lila were by my side and helped me up to my feet. They could only gather bits and pieces of information but obviously knew that something was terribly wrong. I told them there was a helicopter and police dogs looking for Joey. I looked at them with tears pouring down my face and asked them, "It had to be bad, right?" They simultaneously looked at each other for an answer because individually they didn't have one and could not answer me.

My cell phone rang again. It was an old friend of mine, Ronald, "Sheila, are you okay? Where are you at? There's police all over town looking for your son. I heard he shot a cop. Is that true?"

"Oh, my God! What? Shot a cop?" I heard Julia gasp and start crying at those words. "Ronald, that couldn't be true. I just spoke with him, he would have told me… I can't talk anymore." I hit the button on the phone to end the call. I didn't want to hear any more. I had to sit down. As I rocked back and forth in the chair crying, I was saying out loud, "Oh, please, God…what did my baby do? Oh, God, oh, God, oh, God…" It's all I could say. The tears continued to pour from my eyes. My face was red; it must have looked like I had sunburn. My skin felt hot. The blood was rushing throughout my body. I was having trouble breathing and could not catch my breath. This was so surreal; none of this could possibly be true. Julia asked me if I wanted her to drive me home. I could understand she didn't think I would be okay to drive, but I told her I was fine, even though I wasn't. The truth is she was very dear to me and I didn't want to put her in the middle of anything unforeseeable.

Chapter Twenty-Five

I sat there in a chair trying to get my thoughts together. I needed to call the police department to find out exactly why they were searching for my son. "Hello, Peekskill Police Department."

"This is Sheila McGlarry. Can you tell me if it's true the police are looking for my son Joey?"

A voice paused, and sounding as he genuinely felt sympathy for me, the voice said, "Hold on, Sheila. I'll put a sergeant on the phone." There was what seemed like a long pause before I heard a man's voice. A sergeant got on the phone and confirmed that the State Police had called in a search for Joey and that they were using a helicopter and police dogs and that they, the Peekskill Police Department, were just backing them up.

I was shaking, trembling fiercely. This was a mother's worst nightmare. When our children are small we dream- oh, how we dream- how successful our children will be, never once imagining that we will get a phone call from our children running from police dogs, trying to escape from a crime, knowing or maybe not believing that in time it was only inevitable that they would be confined in handcuffs, facing a future of not such success but of deep failure, but maybe we, the parents, on their path, failed them somewhere along the road, that they are running, fleeing, feeling that that was a better choice than facing whatever consequences would be warranted by their actions.

My voice weak, I asked the officer, "Did my son hurt anybody?"

"No. No one was hurt and no weapons were involved."

It didn't make sense to me and there was nothing more he would tell me.

I sat there with my mind racing. Someone was not telling me something. I needed to know what was going on. I couldn't imagine how I was going to do this, how was I going to deal with this from minute to minute. I was trying to think of the first steps I should take, who I should call? My client was sitting there through all this and I'm sure uncomfortably so. I needed somehow to manage to reach down deep for some professionalism to finish her hair, but I was scared and I knew my son had to be even more scared. I needed to know what he did to warrant this massive search if no one was hurt.

I found a few minutes of strength and I stood up. I went over to my client and with each stroke of the flat-iron; tears that rolled down my cheeks would delicately fall off the edge of my jaw bone. She kept saying it was okay, that I didn't need to finish her hair. She said she understood. I couldn't speak or I would fall apart, so I stayed silent and I flat-ironed her hair and let the tears fall one by one.

When I was done I grabbed my keys. Then I had a thought, I turned to Lila, choking back tears, and asked her, "If the police and the news are at my home, can the boys and I come upstate to your house?"

"Of course, you can."

Julia added, "You know you are welcome at ours also." I nodded my head and walked out to my car.

As I was driving home not knowing what to expect, I was remembering a time not that long ago when my neighborhood was swarming with police looking for a young man that lived up the street and how awful it was for his mother. That young man later ended up dying in a police chase.

I thought I'd better call Adam, and let him know what was going on. As his phone was ringing, I was crying at the thought of how do I even begin to tell him. He answered his cheerful, "Hey, what's up?" He knew my silence spoke more than words. "What's wrong, Sheila?"

"I don't even know how to tell you this, but the police are looking for Joey. They have police dogs and they're even using a helicopter. I'm not sure what he did. I called the police but got no direct answer."

There was silence now on his part.

"Are you sure a helicopter is involved?"

"Yes. The police confirmed it because someone had called me saying he shot a cop; the police told me that no weapons were involved but they would not tell me what he did to warrant this. They said that the state police called in the search."

There was more silence and his good mood dissipated into disbelief as he said, "Sheila, this is serious."

And the tears filled my eyes so thick like a river flooding a valley that I couldn't see. "I'm going to grab some clothes maybe and get the boys and then I'm leaving, but I'll call you wherever I end up at, okay."

"Okay. Sheila, be strong. Whatever happens, we will figure this out, okay."

"Okay, bye." I was feeling thankful that we were able to have a strong friendship, especially for our boys.

I called Janna, who was close as a sister to me and always so logical. She answered the phone and immediately said, "Hey, did you get the message that the schools are on lockdown?"

"What? Oh, my God! Janna, I have to tell you it's because the police are looking for Joey."

"What?" she yelled into the phone to me.

"Yes. It's so surreal. Have you seen or heard a helicopter flying around?"

"Oh, my God, Sheila, yes! What happened? What did he do?"

"Listen, I'm nervous about staying at the house. Can we come over there for a little while and I'll tell you what I know when I get there?"

"Of course come over."

"Okay, I'm just going to go grab A.J. from school and then I'll be right there."

All I could think of was my fear, my fear that penetrated through every fiber of my being, I was so scared, and then I thought of my Joey's fear. He was so fearful; I heard it in his voice. And he called me because he was scared, and even though I knew he was selling drugs and kicked him out, he called me. He reached out to me because in the end I am his mother and I am the one person he can call anytime no matter what. That's what I told him growing up, that no matter what, good, bad, right or wrong, he was my child and I would always be there for him.

My head was pounding from thinking and from crying. I called his cell phone and he answered, "Are you okay, Mom?"

"No, Joey I'm not okay. Where are you? I'm very scared for you right now. What's going on? Please explain to me why the police are looking for you. Are you going to turn yourself in?"

"Mom, I am, but I want you with me. I can't talk right now. I'll call you when I'm ready." He paused and then he said he loved me. I wanted to tell him I loved him too but the phone went dead.

After a minute or two, I sent Anthony a text message and told him to go to Janna's house after school. I went to pick up A.J. and I walked directly to the office, not wanting to make eye contact with anyone since my eyes were swollen from crying.

A.J. was excited to see me, as he usually was which was an incredible feeling to see his face light up every time his eyes would see me. As soon as he got in the car, he blurted out, "Mom, some kids didn't have recess today and they weren't allowed outside because the police were searching for someone who escaped." I had to fight back my tears and ask him how the rest of his day was. I couldn't begin to think of how I would tell him what was going on. How would I tell the boys that the lockdown in the schools was because the man the police were searching for was their brother? I knew I would have to tell them because eventually it would be heard throughout the school.

We went straight to Janna's house and she made some coffee. While the boys played, we talked. After I was all cried out and had calmed down and thought about everything, I decided to go home. I needed to be home. If Joey went to the house, I needed to be there for him.

As I came around the corner, there were no cars, no news team, no police, so I pulled in and parked the car. When I went in the house, I closed the blinds, which would stay closed for a while. I made a cup of tea and took two Tylenol for my pounding headache. As I lifted the teabag up and down into the hot water, I thought about all the things I had been through with this kid in his short life. My thoughts were interrupted by the loud sound of the helicopter above me. I went out the front door and looked above as it continued in its search for my son. I thought to prepare myself to tell the boys, but I wasn't ready right now and for their sake it could wait a little longer.

I called Joey's cell phone but it was off and kept going right to voicemail. I left him a message telling him I loved him and somehow we would get through this.

Thursday was a day full of emotional turmoil. I called his phone all morning and it still went directly to voicemail.

I kept calling his phone, which was now ringing, but he was not answering. Finally, after a dozen calls to his phone, he answered in a sarcastic tone, "What?"

"Joey, we need to talk."

He hung up. I called back and he wouldn't answer. I called and I called and I called, and finally, he answered yelling into the phone, "Ma, what do you want? Stop calling me! Are you trying to track me?" I was stunned as I heard the click of the phone. I cried. I didn't understand the animosity towards me.

I was in a daze most of the day. Anthony had come home from school and wanted to know what happened with Joey because all the kids in school were asking him why the police were looking for him and he wanted to know if it was true that the lockdown in school the day before was because of Joey. I embraced him and apologized for not telling him sooner. The tears rolled down my face, as I was unable to hold them back. I thought to myself how stupid I was for not telling him sooner. I sat both the boys down and told them what I knew, which was not much.

I cried on and off, and when Adam came over to see how things were and if I was okay, I cried to him. I was so wrapped up in my own dispirited emotions that I could not see he was also heavyhearted, knowing he had a hand in helping to raise him. He cried because he felt he failed him. The louder he sobbed, the more it made me want to be strong. I saw his pain, I felt every inch of it, and it made me want to stop feeling sorry for myself and it made me want to stop feeling sorry for Joey and deal with whatever the unknown was to be. Adam was not responsible for Joey's bad choices and neither was I.

Friday, I woke up raging mad, wanting and needing control, because my fear was destroying me. I couldn't eat, I couldn't sleep, I could only cry. My son was on the run and I had no idea where he was or who he was with and if he was safe. Someone was not telling me everything. I had no idea what exactly warranted a helicopter search and I knew whatever it was, was beyond anything I could comprehend. I really only knew what the state trooper had said about Joey and Carla shoplifting and that certainly wasn't serious enough for a full-fledged search. I thought it was strange that no police had knocked on the door wanting to know if I had heard anything from my son or even if he was here.

Joey finally called me and apologized for his behavior. He told me he wasn't in town anymore and that he was fine. I told him that I loved him and was very concerned and that we really needed to take care of this before it got any worse.

I called the trooper barracks to find out exactly what was going on and what exactly my son was being charged with. I probably should have done this sooner but in all reality I wasn't thinking too clearly. An officer told me he was being charged with petty larceny and criminal possession of a controlled substance crack-cocaine. My mind was racing, wondering how much drugs he must've had on him that they called in the helicopter search, so I asked him who authorized a helicopter search. After a slight pause, he responded that he didn't know. I asked why it was such a serious search with the use of police dogs for a petty larceny charge. I informed him that the Peekskill Police Department had told me without any reservations that it was the State Police who called for the search and that they were backing them up. He couldn't or wouldn't tell me anything. All he said was that he could not discuss any details with me.

Later in the day, a friend of mine who was in law enforcement, asked me how the relationship between Joey and his father was. I knew without a doubt in my mind, only keeping silence with my thoughts, why there was a helicopter search for my son. He inadvertently confirmed that at some point, someone, between Tuesday and Wednesday morning, recognized that there was a connection between Joey and his father Larry. Someone realized that this was the son of a man who had been investigated for many years by the local police department and the Feds for drug activity and they could never get their hands tight enough on him.

The local paper reported that the State Police claimed there were two escaped prisoners from the county jail to justify the use of police dogs and a helicopter. The paper also stated that they called the Westchester County Jail to confirm the story and the jail had no knowledge of any escaped prisoners and never reported such. I thought of calling the paper and the local news channels but was stopped by my own fears of the publicity and what it would bring to my home, to my children, to his other brothers and sisters on his father's side, as well as my son on the run. I knew Joey could walk into a store, if he were hungry, to get something to eat right now, but if I called to give a story on what I knew and how the taxpayers money was being wasted on an exuberant search for a man they assumed was a major player in the drug world simply based on DNA, his face would be all over the place and then if he were hungry he could not so easily walk into a store.

Tears again came forth as I remembered that night in the supermarket parking lot over 20 years ago when the bag of crack fell from his father's sweatshirt and the choice I made to not want a life with this man for this reason. I knew his children would suffer the consequences of his actions. There would have been no helicopter searches now if not for his name; Joey would have been treated like any other small-time drug dealer or alleged shop-lifter.

Chapter Twenty-Six

On Saturday, the fourth day that my son was on the run, I had gone to work, physically anyway, though mentally my thoughts weighed heavily on my son, his whereabouts, and how his future was starting to look. My concerns ran rampant and I fought very hard to act like my normal happy self and not let the world know my life as a mother was severely troubled.

He must have sensed my worries and eagerness to hear from him or maybe his conscious was telling him to call his mother because about mid day he called to tell me he loved me and that he was okay. I told him I wanted to see him. He was silent for a moment on the phone but then told me to call his cell phone later when I got off work and for me to call Kima.

The day just dragged on and on before I finally got off work. I called Joey's girlfriend and asked her if she wanted to go see Joey with me and she, of course, did. I went to see the boys for a little bit, then I brought them to their dad's house, I packed some groceries for Joey, picked Kima up, and then I called him. It seemed the phone rang forever before he answered. I got nervous he did not want me to see him now, but then he finally answered.

"Hey, Ma. Are you ready?"

"Yes, and I have Kima with me."

"Okay. I'm in Beacon. Call me when you get there. Love you." Click.

About ten minutes after I started driving up to Beacon; a friend who knew about the search for Joey happened to be driving by my house and called me to tell me he didn't see my car and wanted me to know there was a detective car sitting outside my house. I gave him a thank-you and told him I would call him back. I then told Kima what was just told to me and we spoke about how we couldn't believe this was happening and we needed to convince Joey to turn himself in.

When I got to Beacon I pulled over at a gas station and called Joey. He directed me from that point to another, from one light to another, a right turn here, a left turn there, and then I found myself entering a driveway that led up behind a large house. And finally, standing there in the darkness was the silhouette of a man, and as the headlights caught a glimmer of his face I could see it was my son.

I got out and held my arms out to embrace him, a long hug that secured a little faith and hope, a hug that brought a little piece of safety to him that his mother was here like when he was a small child and needed me. I let go and he told me he was glad I was there. I nodded my head and moved out of the way so he could hug his girlfriend.

I grabbed the things I brought him from the car, a coat and a duffle-bag with some clean clothes, deodorant, a toothbrush, and a couple of bags of groceries. He took everything from me and carried it up the stairs, and as I was walking up behind him I knew at this point I was most likely committing a crime, but he was my child and I wanted to do this the right way.

He introduced me to his friend and then we went in the living room to speak privately about everything that had been going on. This was the first time since he'd been on the run that he was finally explaining the events of Tuesday night and Wednesday afternoon to me, and I was ready to listen intently. He told me how he and Carla had gone to the department store, and he had no intention of stealing anything because was able to pay for what he wanted he put a sweater on over his shirt to try on without having to go in the dressing room, Carla, he said, suddenly wasn't around, and a state police officer approached him and asked if he knew where Lost Control was. Joey realized the trooper was being sarcastic, and remembering he had crack-cocaine on him, he took off running out of the store. As he ran out, he remembered the sweater on his back, ripped it off and threw it. He saw Carla walking to her car, where the police followed and arrested her.

The next day Carla called him and asked him to meet her outside on the side of the apartment building that he was staying. Another friend, Arthur, told him not to go, that something didn't seem right, they found drugs in her car yet she was able to drive it. Most people would have had it impounded and had to go through a court process before getting it back so quickly. Because of what his friend said, he went with caution. As he was exiting the building, Arthur said he would hold the automatic-lock door in case Joey needed to run back in. Joey said that as he approached Carla's car she had a weird look on her face and was insistent that he get in the car. He, himself, felt something was off, and as he looked back to Arthur, Arthur was looking in a different direction with a strange look on his face. Joey instinctively turned to see what it was and was shocked to see State Police cars, Peekskill Police cars, and unmarked cars driving from all directions. He knew it was all for him, that he had been set up by his friend Carla. As Arthur was yelling for him to run, an officer pulled his gun and told him not to move or he would shoot, and in an instant Joey decided to run.

As he was running up a one-way street, police cars were driving down past him, unable to stop quick enough and he ran through a park to a nearby school and up behind into a neighborhood full of houses. He heard police dogs barking and running after him. There was a house that sat up high and had a fence enclosure that he leapt over but the dogs could not get through. He was able to run into dense brush up in the hills and away from the houses. The helicopter hovering above was unable to locate him as they circled the west side of the city of Peekskill searching.

By staying in the brush he was able to evade the helicopter and make it all the way to the other side of the city to another apartment complex, where the boys he calls his "brothers" were. They switched clothes with him and hid him until another friend came down and put him under the laundry in his car and they then drove right through a police barricade. That friend took him to another friend's house and yet another friend picked him up and took him to a place to meet another friend, who took him to Beacon. The minute the police went after Joey the way they did, his friends went in motion to help him. They were sure he most likely would have been beaten for making fools of the police if caught.

I couldn't believe what I was hearing. I was overwhelmed at hearing such a story, it was surreal, and I was so grateful to his friends, because we hear about stories like this often on the news. I was grateful for Joey having such friends that would risk their own safety to look out for him, but now I was also fearful of the police. I knew they would want him badly at this point, so I told him he needed to stay there, where it was quiet, until I could retain an attorney the following Monday, then he would have to do the right thing by safely turning himself in, and then we would take it step by step.

It was time for me to go and I told him to stay inside, keep his head together, and that I loved him. I gave him some time to say goodbye to his girlfriend. I can't even describe the feeling of walking out of that apartment and having to leave my son there. I should have been able to bring him home.

The next day, Sunday, I stayed in the house rather numb unable to do anything but think over and over again of the saga Joey relayed to me. I knew he should have turned himself in immediately but I also knew he was scared and he wasn't going to do it so I had no choice but to do it this way. I couldn't alienate him. I had to make him want to do the right thing on his terms. I needed him to feel as though he was in control of his life because scared people do stupid things.

It was later that same night that Kima called me asking me if I could go pick up Joey from the train station. I asked her what she meant and I was scared of what I knew she was obviously going to tell me.

She said he was on the last train down, and as I was throwing a sweatshirt on, I was saying, "Dam-it" to her on the phone. I got to the station before his train and it gave me a minute to think that if Adam knew what I was doing right now he would flip out. I had mixed emotions but I knew I was not about to leave my son to walk the dark streets alone so I could only hope, as a parent, he would understand.

The train came and I got out, I opened the back door of the car, and told him to get down on the floor. I hopped on the highway to drive around the outskirts to get home so no one would see us.

The following Monday I had to go to work and I had to hire an attorney. In the afternoon I thought we would take care of what needed to be taken care of, meaning hire the attorney and have Joey turned in to the police safely. It did not happen. Joey was not ready; he was scared. I thought maybe we should take a day and get our thoughts together. I informed him to lay low in the house and that the next day he would be turning himself in. I had to explain to his brothers that they had to stay inside, they could not have any friends over, and more importantly, they could not tell a soul that their brother was here, not one soul.

On Tuesday I woke him before I left for work and I told him that I made some coffee and that no matter who knocked on the door, not to dare look out through the closed blinds, my car would not be parked outside, so if there was any movement, and someone such as the police would know he was inside. It wouldn't matter who it was, that if it was important, they would come back.

By the time I got home it was late afternoon. Kima had come over with the baby and we were having a last supper of sorts. I hired an attorney and then I told Joey he was going to turn himself in first thing in the morning. He was very nervous, but I made it clear that as a family we were there for him and he was not going to go through this alone.

The next day I got up and got the boys ready for school. Joey was up and he was quieter than he had been the day before. After I dropped them off, I went back to the house to get ready to take Joey. My cell phone was ringing and it was a friend of mine who was a local police officer. I was instantly suspicious, being I hadn't spoken to him in a quite a few months, but I thought it better to answer and see what he had to say. He, of course, asked me how I was doing and said that he had heard what happened.

It was now eight days after the fact and I was sure that he wasn't just hearing about it now, not after a helicopter search was involved and the schools had a lockdown. I didn't say anything, just let him talk. He said that I needed to get Joey to turn himself in. He said that the police were searching for him very hard, knocking on doors starting very early in the morning to find him. I could not tell him he was here so I told him Joey was upstate and he was going to be taking a train down and then would go turn himself in. He suggested that I let his detective friend handle it and stressed that he was a nice guy. As much as I respected him, I had to do this myself, because even though he was a friend, he was a police officer first, and I understood this. We ended our conversation on the note that I would call him when Joey was ready.

Joey was dressed but not ready to go emotionally, he was scared of the unknown, and I couldn't blame him. When I was ready, I went downstairs. I looked at Joey and said, "Let's go kiddo."

"I think I am going to wait a bit…until Kima gets off from work. I want to see the baby."

In a gentle voice I said, "No, you saw the baby last night. Let's go now. It will only be worse in the end if you keep delaying. I've been patient and gave you whatever I thought you needed to prepare for this. I hired an attorney to protect you and your rights, I know you are scared, but nothing will happen to you, and we really need to go. "

He sat there for just a moment, and then stood up looking at me with eyes full of trust. "Okay, let's do this, Mom."

I called Greg -Janna's husband- who was willing to go with us for support. I stopped at a gas station to get Joey a pack of smokes and I even let him smoke in the car. I hopped on the highway again to avoid the local police. Joey had burned a few crosses with some of the local police officers, so I decided not to turn him in locally but took him to the state police instead.

I pulled in the parking lot and parked the car. He got out and smoked another cigarette. I knew this would be difficult for him. He paced, he inhaled, he paced, and he inhaled. I looked at Greg, who knew what I was thinking, so he helped me gently encourage Joey to put out the cigarette and walk in. Joey looked at Greg and put the cigarette on the ground and ground his sneaker into it. He turned to Greg, shook his hand, and said thank-you to him.

Joey walked in and stood in front of the bulletproof glass as Greg and I stood behind him. An officer asked him, "May I help you?"

"Yes, sir, I believe you have a warrant for my arrest." He told him his name and the man looked at him respectfully. He came around to open the door for him. When he opened it, I told him I hired an attorney and they were not to interrogate him. I gave him the name of the attorney and informed the officer the attorney wasn't present due to being in the middle of a trial. He very politely responded with a nod of understanding. He then looked at my baby boy and said kindly enough, "Come on in, Mike."

My son then entered though the big slate gray door.

Chapter Twenty-Seven

Joey was arraigned in court and was held on a fifty thousand dollar bail. So in jail he would sit.

An entire year had gone by and as his release date was approaching, he was hit with another charge while incarcerated of selling drugs to an undercover prior to being arrested on the last charge. That charge had been dropped to a misdemeanor, possession, but he would have to stay incarcerated for another year.

During that time he was beaten up by a Westchester County correction officer for saying something sarcastic to him. The officer, who did lose his job over this incident, locked in all the inmates on that block and beat my son and continued to beat my son while handcuffed (in his head) where he now has permanent eye damage and some other issues.

Thank God for two officers who came on the scene and intervened and also did the right thing by not covering it up in the investigation simply because he was a fellow officer and because my son was an inmate which happens way too often. We hired an attorney and filed a multi-million dollar law suit against the officer and the county for failing to protect my son. Westchester County allowed this officer to continue interaction with inmates when he was allegedly known for this kind of behavior, which is just appalling. The county has since installed numerous cameras in the area of the jail where my son was attacked.

Joey was released November of 2010 and I let him move home. He had a part time job and met a new girlfriend. A couple of months had gone by and they started arguing; he eventually quit his job, and started to lose weight. I had noticed he had a second cell phone, and asked him directly if he were selling drugs. He caught an instant attitude and made me feel as if I were jumping to conclusions simply because he had another phone. I knew before I knew. That's why I asked.

By the end of June, Joey had been home for seven months and on the 22d, he called me at work.

"Mom, there are detectives outside the house and I am scared. What should I do?"

I was silent, composing myself since I was at work but I really wanted to scream in to the phone, "What the fuck!" Instead I said, "What are you talking about? What did you do?"

"I didn't do anything."

"You did something…"

"Mom, I didn't do anything."

"Then you have nothing to be afraid of. Go open the door and see what they want."

"Mom, more police cars are outside."

My cell phone went off with a text alert from a neighbor and when I read it, it said, "I thought you should know there are many Peekskill police, Westchester County police and unmarked cars outside your house and the police are surrounding it."

"Joey, I just received a text saying they are surrounding the house. What did you do?"

"Mom, Mom, I don't know!" With that I heard the toilet flush.

"Joey, what are you doing?"

"I was flushing whatever weed I had down the toilet."

"Joey, you need to go outside and see what they want, because you clearly did something and you are fucking lying to me! The police are not surrounding my house for some fucking weed! Go outside before they kick the fucking door in."

"Okay, okay. Mom I'm going out. I love you."

After the call was disconnected, I put the phone back on the receiver and took a deep breath. My eyes filling with tears for the millionth time, my friend Julia said, "What's wrong?"

I answered in a tone of voice that I was sure clearly proved I was fed up, "Joey, what else? What the fuck! I hate to sound so abrasive but when does it fucking end!"

She just said, "Oh, no!" It almost made me laugh.

He was arrested for two counts of criminal sale of a controlled substance in a city-wide drug sweep by the Westchester County Police, state police and City of Peekskill Police. He was brought to Rikers Island Correction Facility in Manhattan, one of the worst jails in the country. I bailed him out on a $10,000 bail that Friday and I drove him immediately up to my mother's house in Orange County.

I was enormously disappointed in him and on the drive upstate we had a conversation about his immediate future and the things he would definitely have to do, achieve, and acquire if he wanted to have any chance at a decent future. This was it. It wasn't even a matter of enough being enough. He was facing serious charges, again, but this time I was sure the penalty would be much more severe. I was calm but firm in telling him that if he got in any more trouble, not to call me, I didn't want to know anything. It was a long, silent car ride and all the while wondering what was wrong with me that I bailed him out.

Joey and my mother came down to Peekskill to my house the following Thursday to get some more of his things. He came in with an attitude, looking for a problem, making sarcastic statements, trying to lure me into an argument. I hadn't seen this behavior in quite some time but recognized it all too well. He wanted to dance, he wanted to spar and this time I would not respond. I told the boys to not respond either.

Anthony sensed it, too. He had planned to go up to his grandmother's house for a few days to hang out with them but changed his mind instantly because he also knew Joey wanted to dance and knew he needed a partner, and wanted no part of it.

Joey was making hurtful, nasty comments here and there. I couldn't get my things together quick enough. He went into his bedroom and made a statement that I couldn't wait to get rid of him. I told him nicely that was not the case but that his stuff, yes, was packed simply because I knew he would need it, as he would no longer continue to live here. As he and I had discussed.

He went downstairs. Anthony ran outside to remove himself from any impending situation, but Joey's eyes followed him, as they always did, then he went out as well. He looked at Anthony and all of a sudden had pulled the earring right out of his ear. Anthony stunned, asked him why he did that and Joey, without cause, punched him in the face. While A.J. was getting his shoes on, I was thinking of getting the heaviest thing I could find to smash Joey with, but instead I decided to stay as calm as I possibly could, not responding and quickly put my things in the car to get out of this situation as soon as possible.

My mother had been quiet; I believe hoping that by nobody saying anything Joey would quiet down. My neighbor was walking her dog and was Joey was now screaming at Anthony for no reason, saying he was a loser and that he would never amount to anything. Joey then screamed at the neighbor, "What the fuck are you looking at?" I was mortified.

Joey started yelling at Anthony again, who had been trying to slide away slowly, and as A.J. was coming around the passenger side of the car, he said to Joey, "Why don't you leave him alone. Get your own life together before you put down someone else," this coming from an eleven year old! I knew he was right, but it was a mistake at this time for anyone to say anything to Joey. Sure enough, Joey went flying around the car as if he was going to now hit A.J., screaming at him that he was a loser, too. He was projecting everything he felt about himself onto everyone else. I shoved A.J. into the car and told him to lock the door. I walked around the back of the car to get to the driver's side. As I was getting into the car I looked over to my mother, who was standing outside her driver's side door, and I told her, "I am done." Joey flipped out.

First, he kicked my car. I started locking the doors from the inside. He ran in front of the car screaming and cursing some more. He had rage burning in his eyes. They were searching for Anthony, who was about a hundred feet down the street now. I raced to start the car. When Joey spotted Anthony, he ran after him. Anthony had no clue, as his back was to him as he walked away. I drove quickly towards Anthony. I knew this time would be different. Joey's rage would be more severe. Joey came within about ten feet of him when he suddenly tripped; it was as if God had tripped him! I thought for a moment that maybe he had broken something, but in that moment I didn't care, I just needed to get Anthony in the car, away from Joey and his violent outburst.

I pulled the car up and begged Anthony to get in while Joey lay motionless on the ground. Anthony looked back at him and then walked over to see if he was okay. He put his hand on Joey's back, and whatever Joey said to him, Anthony walked away crying. He wiped away each tear with a hard stroke, a combination of questioning himself if he were emotionally hurt or angry... wondering why Joey treated him this way, wondering what he did to deserve this treatment from him, wondering what he did to deserve any of the outburst Joey had directed at him over the years.

I kept asking him to get in the car, and he would not answer me but only walk further away while I followed next to him driving the car slowly. Finally, I stopped the car and got out.

"Anthony, you need a hug. Let me give you a hug baby. I need a hug Anthony, you are hurting and it's killing me."

He looked at me and we walked towards each other, the tears now swelling in his eyes and spilling out of him as he got closer to me, and as my arms reached for him, he embraced me letting all the pain release through his tears. I held my son, my very sad sobbing son. I told him I was so upset that Joey behaved this way, he didn't deserve it. I promised him I would never let this happen to him again. He just cried in my arms. And the tears poured out of me while I held him close to me.

Sheila McGlarry

Afterword

To have a child is one of the greatest gifts we are given in this world and the love that we are granted is the greatest of any love known, purely unconditional.

When our child has fallen into a world of addiction, no matter what kind it may be, we as the parents are ridiculously blinded by our love and crippled by our own addiction to denial, because we without a doubt, love our child more than our own life, and our mind just doesn't allow us to see the destruction that has crept in to our life, and that, that has taken that precious child and made him or her imperfect in the most obscure way.

In writing this book, I was able to release my thoughts, anxieties, fears, hopes, my forgotten aspirations and failures as a parent. It was difficult to talk to my family, friends, or co-workers about this. It meant I had to admit my son was not perfect. It meant I was not the perfect parent. It meant I had to admit my son was an addict. It meant I should have been able to save him and couldn't. It meant I had to admit that only he could choose to save himself. It meant I was powerless. What unbearable thoughts for any parent to have, thoughts that have brought me to tears many, many nights.

There are a few things I would like readers to get from this book, one of them being, if you are going through this, you are not alone. Reach out for help or guidance. It is so important to have some form of support. I myself get strength by talking to other parents and helping them in whatever way I can.

The denial that we embrace so warmly, is the denial that we have to let go of for our child but more so for our self. There are signs, there are so many signs that we ignore, justify, or make excuses for and we can't afford to anymore because we are losing our children. And quite frankly if parents, care givers, guardians, teachers, even neighbors, see signs of drug or alcohol abuse, it needs to be addressed on the spot. We need to go back to the old saying, "It takes a village." Do you hear me? It does take a village.

We first and foremost must educate our children. We are not giving them the education they deserve. We have to give them an academic foundation to help them thrive and we have to give them life skills. I believe we also have to give them a religious or spiritual foundation which instills a conscience. We have to give them unconditional love.

I read somewhere, "We have to prevent. If we prevent, we don't have to intervene."

There are so many foundations that can help. Here in Peekskill there is the Elton Brand Foundation, an after school program that gives free tutoring to the teens as well as extra-curricular activities and support to single parent homes. Family Ties, is an organization that helps in the support of families with children with various issues. The Peekskill Police Youth Cadet Program, which has a two week summer camp as well an afterschool program for kids interested in law enforcement, and the City of Peekskill Youth Bureau, have programs set up for city kids up to age 21 to help them become positive and successful. They help in the prevention and intervention of families in need. There are organizations like these in most communities. You can search through a school counselor, local police departments, or your church or synagogue.

Nationwide there is the Lea Black Foundation which focuses on prevention, and intervention of at risk kids. There is A.A., N.A., and Al-Anon, Big Brothers/Big Sisters, The Steve and Marjorie Harvey Foundation which has programs such as, Mentoring for Young Men, Girls Who Rule the World, and Scholarship Opportunities. There is the National Guard Youth Foundation which helps troubled teens turn their life around. These are just a few; there are so many more organizations out there to help.

Whether you are the troubled teen reading this book, an addict, an inmate, or the loved one in angst, I cannot stress enough that there is help out there; you just have to extend your hand and someone will grab it and not let go.

The one thing I've learned is that no matter what the religious, racial, demographic or economic background, the pain and the blame are all the same. As I wrote this, I cried through paragraphs and I sobbed through each chapter as my fingers typed painful emotions, reliving it and realizing what I have accepted, and even more painfully how long it took me.

There are so many stories like mine, hundreds, thousands, hundreds of thousands, and each one is unique, but I bet, each one has that one thing in common, that being denial. Being a parent that remained in denial until I couldn't anymore because I was riddled with such extreme guilt and pain, blaming myself and by the time it was realized and or accepted, I acted too late.

Give your child faith, faith in the love that their parent has for them, faith that no matter what he or she does in life, no matter how severe the mistake, they know without a doubt that you love him or her unconditionally. And maybe when the strings start to come untied in their lives, they might have the faith and strength to come to you for help in securing the knot instead of hanging from it. Do everything you can do as a parent to save them. Even if you can't, you have to try, no matter how ugly it gets, no matter how dark and grim and never-ending it seems. No matter to what extreme lengths you have to go.

And then sometimes with immense sadness I admit after all has failed it means letting go. I have had to let go. I have had to exercise what some call tough love. Sometimes ironically that's what you have to do to save your child. Sometimes the fear of an addict losing his or her family might just be enough for them to reach out for help and sometimes it isn't, but either way you cannot continue to live your life in pain, and at some point you just have to move forward with your own life and accept that you cannot change the person.

County jails and state prisons are filled with young males and young women who should instead be in college or working and experiencing life at a time when life is supposed to be experienced and explored. Joey at this point was facing quite a few years in state prison. The thought was unbearable to me and I could not even fathom the harsh reality of a prison life for him if he were convicted. But these were the choices he made and he would be inevitably accountable to such.

Acknowledgements

This was such a painful journey for me, as well as for my family and some very close friends. I am sure it might even be painful for many readers as they can relate to the words and to the pain they have experienced with their own loved one whose has/had an addiction or any other type of issue that affects the family unit. The road traveled is long and heart-wrenching I know.

There are so many people I want to thank and can only hope each person knows how much he or she mean to me.

First I want to that the Lord for guiding me and giving me a voice that might help save a family. For giving me the strength I needed that at times I wasn't aware I had.

I want to thank my beautiful mother, there really are no words to express the love and gratitude I have for you. Thank you for teaching me about God from such a young age and what it means to have faith. For loving me unconditionally in all my own errs. Thank you for encouraging me to tell this story and showing me that it is not just a book about the addict and addiction but the denial in the enabler and that the cycle has to stop.

Maybe, I am hoping something will click in someone's mind and as they read these words right now, at this very moment, they are realizing they are in denial and their child has a significant problem. I am hoping right now, at this second, they are putting the book down to call someone, or searching to find an Al-Anon meeting, or a Family Ties Organization to get the support that is needed.

I want to thank Family Ties in Peekskill, NY. You gave me guidance, strength and hope.

Amin, you entered my life when Joey was a young boy and you helped me to raise him, which wasn't easy and in spite that maybe the stress was just too much and our relationship failed, I do feel blessed that we have been fortunate enough to find and maintain a friendship and still co-parent together. I do hope you know you are an amazing father.

Jennifer M., you and your family have become our extended family, have been nothing but supportive and amazing with the boys in helping to keep them stable and positive, excepting them with nothing but immense love; for that I am forever thankful.

My dear friend Jennifer L., her husband Craig, and her four beautiful children who give great hugs, I shed many tears with you and at times listened to harsh advice that was hard to swallow, but choked down over many cups of coffee and I love you for it and your beautiful family.

I want to thank my friend David M. for always being there when I would write an e-mail that went on and on with me venting at 3A.M. and how I would tell you no need to reply back, but you would always reply with not always what I wanted to hear, but what I needed to hear and also with wonderful words of support.

To my sweetest friend June, I am so sorry for making you cry. Every time I'd cry, you would cry more.

You are always supportive. If I wanted to talk, I could talk. If I just wanted to sit and be quiet you would just sit and be quiet next to me. I love you dearly and no matter where I am in this world, I am only a thought away.

Angela, probably one of my oldest friends who was right there when I gave birth to that sweet little boy and how you let me squeeze your hand so tight that you lost feeling in it for days. That is true friendship. I want to thank you for telling me not words of advice of what I should do as a parent with my son but what I needed to do for myself as a woman and parent. You are the sister I never had.

Erina, Louise, Rita, Lucia, Andre, Diane R., Lisa, Tom F., Kenny, John, Siobhan, Jason, Ebony, Ana, Robert, Doug, Maxine, Nicole, Diane, Nivia, Kat, Francis, Robin, Denise, Trudy, Chris, Ms. Virginia, thank you all for being such wonderful people and friends who did not pass judgment, only encouraged me not to quit on him and always rooted for my son a long side of me.

To everyone who knew when it was weighing heavily on me but gave me my space when I couldn't talk about it.

To the Mahopac Writers Group, I cannot thank you all enough. To each and every writer in this group you are all talented writers, incredible listeners and amazing people.

This group was my saving grace. Writing has always been a passion of mine but when I started writing this I didn't know I was writing it. When the first chapter was read, I knew the story had to be written, when the second chapter was read, I knew the story had to be shared. Thank you for the all the advice, what was too much information, what was not enough. Dana... Thank you for being an amazing editor and also for all your wonderful suggestions.

To Margi Picciano, my formatting trouble shooter, I truly appreciate your time and patience, thank you. Andy.... The group wouldn't be a group without you. You make sure everyone is well informed and kept up to date with what is going on in the community with writer events.

A very special thanks to Vincent Dacquino for first creating the Mahopac Writer's Group and secondly for being a wonderful friend and writing coach to me, I really need to thank you for encouraging me that this story needed to be told. Especially on days when I thought it was too raw and too personal and helping me to realize that this story is what parents and loved ones of addicts or troubled teens needed to see. So many feel they are alone in their heartache or too embarrassed and ashamed, feeling like a failure as a parent and sadly they don't realize how many of us there are.

Janus Adams, your grace, talent and professionalism as an author is something every writer aspires to be. Every time you heard a part of my story you enriched me with such positive feedback, I knew I was doing the right thing. Thank you for your advice and guidance.

To the City of Peekskill Police Department, there are a few of you who I built relationships with over the years and to know that you truly wished Mike well and rooted for him to get through his difficult time and that there were times you could have arrested him but did not, knowing that wasn't necessarily the answer. Officer Jones, you have been to my home a dozen times, maybe more and the patience that you exhibit in resolving whatever issue of the day it was had a profound effect on me as a parent and on my son's life. Officer Esposito, thank you for just reaching out to Joey when you would see him around or if he were in police custody you would always just talk to him. Lt. Kathy Johansen, thank you for our chats, they truly meant a lot to me. Officer Dylewski, thank you for genuinely caring and always checking up on us. Thank you for listening to me, I am glad we became friends. Officer Le'Perch, thank you for always wishing my son well and hoping for the best.

      I cannot thank enough Ms. Brenda Heady-DiDomenico for your creative talent in helping me to design the book cover. You are so very gifted. You were so easily able to bring to life the title. You are an amazing artist and more of an amazing friend, thank you.

www.ravenswindart.webs.com

      Now to the three most important people in my life, my sweet son A.J., you are an old soul and full of devotion and love for your brothers and family. As I would cry through this process, your hugs helped ease my pain. Always keep that kind, beautiful spirit you were blessed with because not just I but the world has been blessed with you.

My handsome Anthony, this was a difficult road for me and I sometimes wonder if it was more so for you. I pray that one day you and Joey will be able to move forward and be able to love each other and have somewhat of a decent relationship without resentments. Just know that I love you immensely my sweet child.

Joey, my beautiful son, maybe now that you are a father to twins you will understand how much I love you. The choices a parent makes are not always easy but the choices I made for you were always, unconditionally out of love. Thank you for supporting me in writing this. I say to you as well, I love you immensely.

I know there are some deeply personal topics that were addressed but part of that is about it being truthfully raw so it will get through to people. If this book helps families to open their eyes to teenage drinking and drugging, and if it helps to save a child from addiction, or a young man from making the bad choice to sell drugs and ending up in jail, or a parent from denial so they take steps to intervene in their child's life then maybe it was worth it.

Though our relationship is not perfect I am thankful that we are on the path to having a healthier relationship. I am here to encourage you on your worst day so that you will have better days. Put your trust in God. Put faith in yourself that your young life is starting anew.

Present Day

As of October, 2012 Joey has been attending an out-patient program where he gets tested every week as well as checks in with a Judge-in court- on a weekly basis to make sure he is staying on a positive path and when he completes the program she has him in and he proves to her that he is refraining from doing and selling drugs she is going to dismiss his two felony charges and he will have a second chance to change the direction of his future.

This judge has helped in trying to save my son's precious life and others by giving them this opportunity and I cannot thank her enough because this Drug-Court Program gives men and women an opportunity to change the direction of their lives.

There is a "however," if he messes up this incredible opportunity she has given him; he will be brought back into custody and will face the two felonies in court and without a doubt he will be sentenced to state time.

He has met and is now living with someone very special to him and they have just recently given birth to twins. He has been trying to re-build his relationship with his younger brothers. A.J. the younger one is more open to be accepting and forgiving. He loves going over to Joey's house and hanging out with him and spending as much time with him as possible.

Anthony, I think it is going to take him a little more time before he can trust his older brother. But it is what it is and Joey just has to accept that and take baby steps. But I believe in time they will be fine.

As for myself, Joey and I have our differences and we most likely always will. I continue to pray for him every day and hope that he stays on the positive path he is on. I will support him in every way I can because I know, and am very well aware that I am one of the lucky ones who has not buried my child. And for that I thank God every day.

On a final note, I cannot stress enough to parents if you feel something is off with your child, something is.

Alcohol, prescription pills, marijuana, heroine, crystal meth, cocaine, crack-cocaine, huffing with paint, markers, gas, and pcp also known as angel dust, are all easily accessible to our kids.

Many people have this idiotic notion that only "bad" kids or kids with no supervision or no families do drugs. A reality check for you is that even the best of kids who come from the nicest families or who excel in sports or get the best grades do, do drugs. If you see sudden changes no matter how mild in your child, pay attention very closely.

Joey might have personal battles with himself quite possibly for the rest of his life but he has a life and people who care immensely for him, so as long as he continues to make positive choices he, we, will be able to get through anything.

I have to add that I have changed most names. I also would like to add that all the events and dates that I've written about are true to the best of my knowledge. Some of the quotes in conversation might not be word for word but for the most part they are very accurate.

Sheila McGlarry

Please feel free to e-mail me at sheilamcglarry@gmail.com

God Bless.

Made in the USA
Lexington, KY
19 January 2013